book series
Brain Club

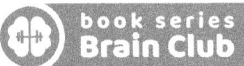

Brain Club

How to Treat and Train Our Brain to Enhance Cognitive Functions

Hamed Ekhtiari, MD, PhD
Tara Rezapour, PhD

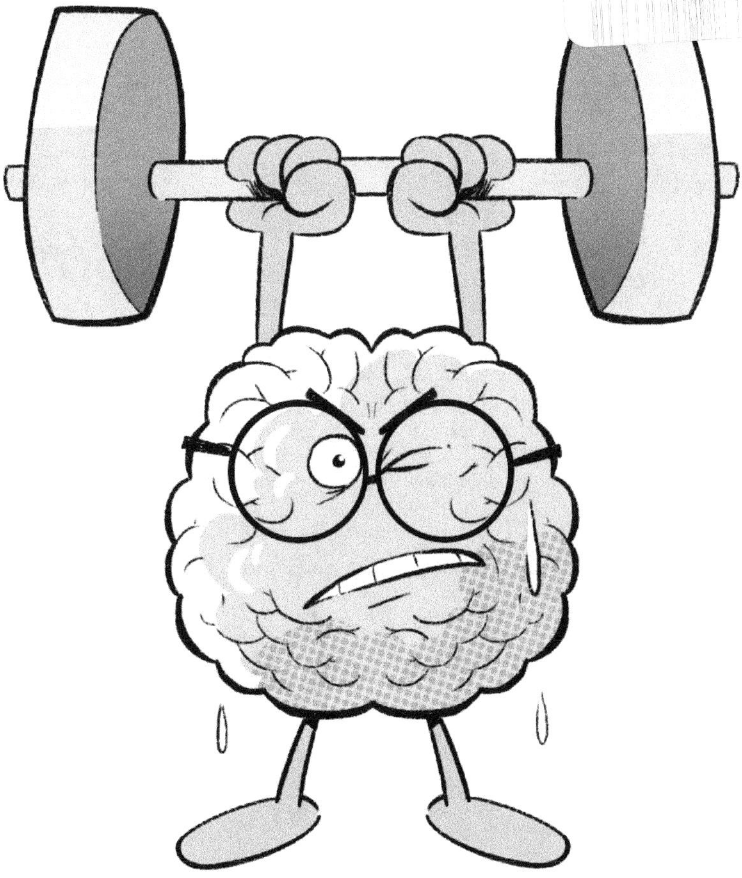

Brain Club

Self Help Work Book
Graded Cognitive Training Exercises

Published by	Metacognium LLC
Authors	Hamed Ekhtiari, Tara Rezapour
Contributors:	Brad Collins, Robin Aupperle Martin Paulus
Illustrator	Naeem Tadayon
Production Manager	Masoome Garshasbi
Art Director	Mohsen Farhadi
Co-Illustrators	Mahdi Ajani, Hesam Talae, Elham Eslam
Graphic Designer	Arash Sarikhani
ISBN	978-1-7347408-1-3

Copyright © 2022 by Metacognium LLC. All rights reserved. This book may not be reproduced, in whole or in part, including illustrations, in any form (beyond that copyright permitted by Sections 107 and 108 of the U.S. Copyright Law and except by reviewers for the public press), without written permission from the publisher. This book is written based on the latest findings in cognitive neuroscience and authors have tried their best to make it as accurate and up to date as possible. However, it may contain errors, oversights, or materials that is out of date at the time you read it. The authors and publisher disclaim any legal responsibility or liability for errors, oversights, and out-of-date materials, or the reader's application of the information or advice contained in this book. The material of this book is not intended to replace the services of your physician, therapist, or caregiver. Since the recovery process for each person is unique, you should consult with your own physician or therapist to evaluate the symptoms you may have, or to receive suggestions for appropriate interventions.

Addiction Treatment
and Recovery Center
12&12
www.12and12.org

metacognium™
www.metacognium.com

Laureate
Institute for
Brain Research
www.laureateinstitute.org

Contents

1st Session	9
2nd Session	25
3rd Session	41
4th Session	57
5th Session	73
6th Session	89
7th Session	105
8th Session	121
9th Session	137
10th Session	153
11th Session	169
12th Session	185
13th Session	201
14th Session	217
15th Session	233
16th Session	249
Answer	265

Introduction

Imagine that you have just gotten the cast removed from your broken arm. You feel so happy to return your life as it was before the injury. But as soon as you try to get move your arm, you find that it is not as easy as before. The muscles are too weak to control your arm movement. Your doctor prescribed a course of physical therapy sessions with focus on physical exercises to strengthen your arm muscles and improve your functional movements. Each session would offer a regular and structured set of exercises under your therapist's supervision. Once a set is successfully completed, you can start the new one with a higher level of difficulty. Gradually, you will see that you are able to move your arm faster and more fluently. This is the benefit of physical therapy with an essence of your commitment

The above scenario of a broken arm is similar to what happens in the brain for people with substance use disorders who decide to start the treatment course. During the first few weeks of abstinence and detoxification, the brain is very much like the broken arm that needs to be in peaceful condition without any stress. But after reaching a medically stable point, it's time to start strengthening exercises. For this type of healing, we offer a series of brain exercises instead of physical therapy.

Brain exercises are designed to improve different brain functions in a systematic and structured manner over a specific time period. These exercises begin at a relatively easy level and gradually proceed to the more difficult and challenging levels. The engaging exercises not only activate the brain functions as a part of therapeutic intervention but also turn treatment into a more enjoyable process by offering a bit of fun through the game-based exercises. The main point here is that when using these exercises, patients should be committed to practice them throughout the course of treatment. Naturally therapeutic supervision is important to help track the changes and give patients proper feedback and also encourage them to stay in treatment. But, the most important influence into being successful in this treatment is your personal commitment and motivation for brain recovery.

Brain Club could be considered a brain fitness gym, that once you "join", you will become a member of the club and committed to attend regular sessions. Each session takes around 1 hour and it is better to do the exercises along with other people who are in recovery as group support. But, you can also practice the exercises without being in a group setting. After each group session, there is a homework assignment that should be done individually. Each session targets 2-3 brain functions and these functions will improve with repeated exercises. The target functions are:

1. Attention: The ability to stay focused and concentrate on important information and ignore the irrelevant ones is a brain function called attention. At the optimal level of this functioning, you can read a newspaper in a noisy room or actively participate in a discussion despite potential distractions without missing any important information.

2. Visuospatial processing: "Turning right or left?" sometimes when we want to help other people to find an address, we may inadvertently point in the wrong direction. Visuospatial function is the brain's ability to perceive and mentally manipulate objects as well as identify and recognize spatial information (e.g., spatial direction). Imagine you are going to explore a new place in your city. As much as you need a map and a compass, you need an optimal level of visuospatial functioning.

3. Working memory: "4856…? What was the last number? I have just heard it, why I cannot remember it?" Have you experienced this too? It's because our working memory isn't function-

ing well in early abstinence. Working memory is like our brain's desk. Our brain places the most recent information we received on this desk to be called upon in short intervals. Working memory has a close relationship with attention. When you need to focus on a new piece of information, properly working memory can save it accurately.

4 Verbal skills: The other brain functions that help us to generate verbal concepts appropriate to a specific situation. Verbal skill is a critical function for communication in order to comprehend what other people say and to inform us how to answer them appropriately.

5 Executive functions: Last but not least, are the set of functions generally called executive functions including planning, problem solving, flexibility and response inhibition. Executive functions are necessary for goal-directed behaviors. With an optimal level of executive functioning, we can suppress our impulsive actions and replace them with more planned-out decisions.

On the next page, you can find how we have covered all these 5 functions with different exercises with different levels of difficulty (1 to 5).

Now you are aware of what you might expect in our Brain Club. You also have an idea how to use it under your therapist's supervision. So, time for action: Grab your pencil, set your timer for the first exercise and begin! . We hope you all enjoy the Brain Club.

Cognitive Modules		Sessions	1	2	3	4	5	6	7	8	9	10	11	12	13	14	15	16
Executive functions		Sequencing						1	2	3	4	5					Review	Review
		Finding logical relation						1	2	3	4	5						
		Soduku						1	2	3	4	5						
		Tower of Hanoi					1	2	3	4		5						
		Numerical logic puzzles						1	2	3	4	5						
Verbal skills		Writing story						1	2	3	4	5						
Working memory		Crosswords (Classic Scramble)						1	2	3	4	5						
		Picture recalling						1	2	3	4	5						
		Word recalling						1	2	3	4	5						
Visuospatial process		Maze				1	2	3	4	5								
		Drawing symmetrical side				1	2	3	4	5								
		Puzzles				1	2	3	4	5								
		Mental rotation				1	2	3	4	5								
		Spatial direction				1	2	3	4	5								
Attention		Trial making				1	2	3	4	5								
		Similar / different objects				1	2	3	4	5								
		Letter / number cancelation				1	2	3	4	5								
		Stroop tasks	1	2	3	4	5											
		Finding hidden objects	1	2	3	4	5											
		Spot the differences	1	2	3	4	5											

Brain Club
1st Session

 **Brain Education**

1 Do alcohol/other drug users have different brains even before starting to use drugs?

There is no certain answer for this question, since we do not have enough reliable evidence in the field, yet. While some preliminary studies suggest there is no difference between drug users and non-drug users' brains before starting to use drugs, other researches propose that there are some genetic and environmental factors that may change brain structures and functions in a way that increase one's susceptibility to use drugs or become dependent. For example, childhood adversity or genetic backgrounds for lack of impulse control are among plausible factors in this field. Although, it should be noted that having these risk factors do not necessarily lead to drug use.

2 Do different drugs injure my brain in different ways/areas or do they target the same brain areas and create the same injuries?

There is relative consensus for common aspects of brain injuries caused by different drugs as we demonstrated in the first part of this book. Attention, memory, decision and control, movement and speech, brain-body connection, arousal and sleep, feeling bad, feeling good, social cognition and awareness and insight are the ten most important brain functions which are commonly found impaired among users with different types of drugs. Although it should be noticed that the severity of injuries may be different and also each drug may lead to further specific impairments. For example, in alcohol users, memory deficits are worse than other types of substances and they usually experience more deficits in visual processing in complex environments.

Brain Exercises (Main Session)

We would recommend you to use a stopwatch or simply a watch or a cellphone to record the amount of the time you spend to complete exercises in each session.

 1 Try to find all hidden items in the picture and circle them.

⚠ Attention: You may not find all the hidden items in the picture. It is totally fine. But, we expect you to activate your sustained attention for 10 minutes searching for the hidden items. This activation is our main goal in the brain club. You can find the answers after this session of brain work-out at the end of the book. After finishing the exercises in this session, you may like to be back and color these figures as you like to reduce your tensions.

2 Try to find all hidden items in the picture and circle them.

3 In this exercise, you can see different pictures of animals labeled with a word. In some cases, the labeled word may be congruent with the picture, while in some others they are incongruent. For the first part of the exercise, read just the words, but for the second part accurately name pictures regardless of the written words. Record your time for both parts and compare them.

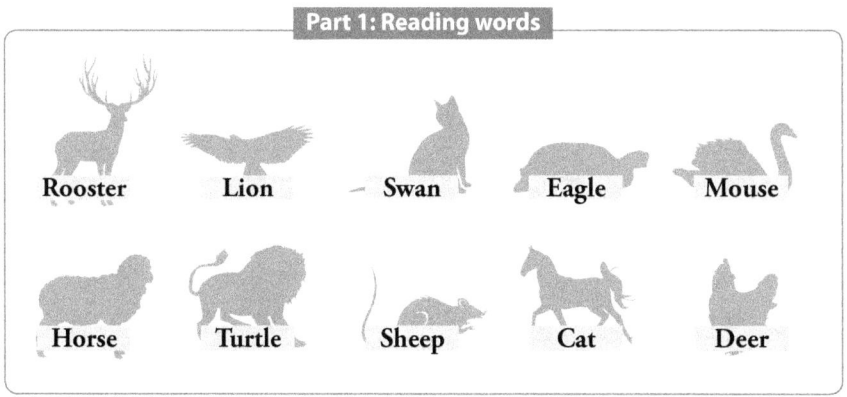

Time (sec):   Number of errors:

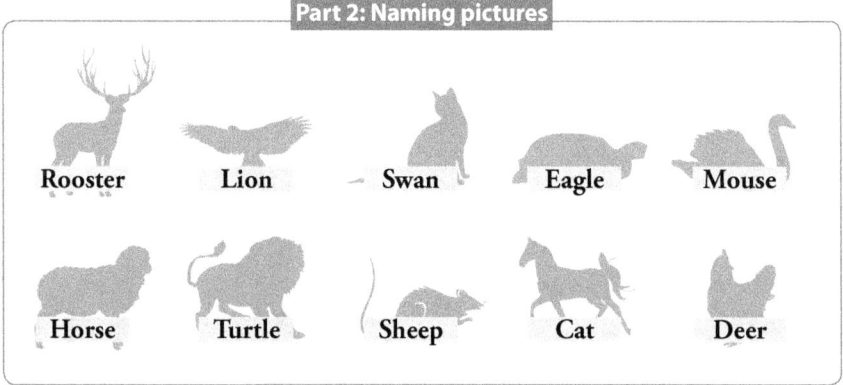

Time (sec):   Number of errors:

4 Look at the below faces and try to identify the emotion conveyed in each face.

5 Scan the below image and try to find as many as target pictures (images with same direction) without marking anything on the paper. Write the total number.

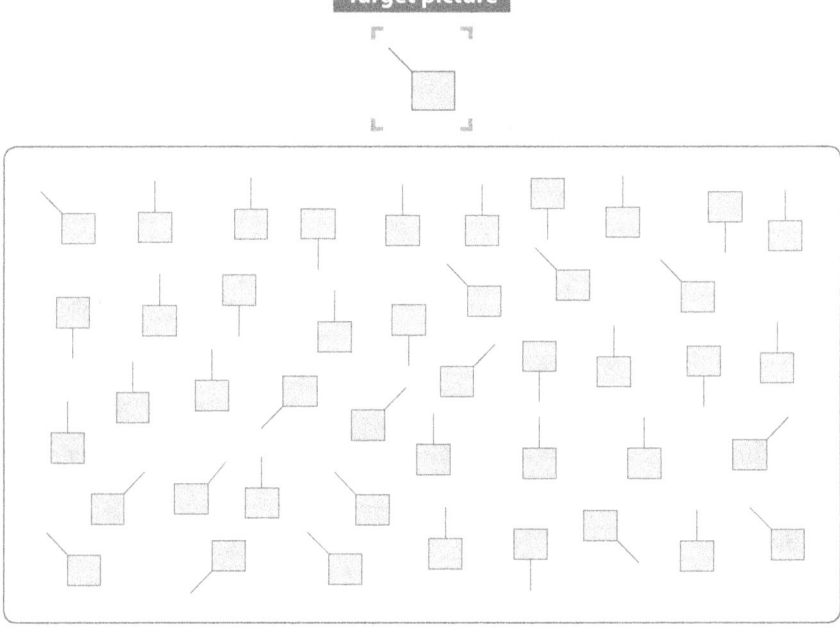

Total number: ....

6 Look carefully at the next three pairs of images below and try to spot differences.

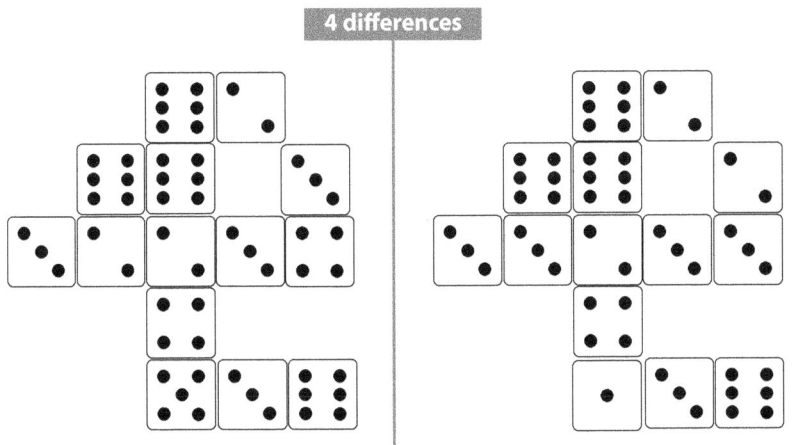

5 differences

 7 Calculate equations below and write the answeres.

a. 80 - 20 =

b. 10 + 15 =

c. 15 + 6 =

d. 40 - 22 =

e. 70 - 22 =

f. 4 × 4 =

g. 8 × 1 =

h. 15 + 9 =

i. 66 ÷ 6 =

j. 15 + 5 =

k. 30 ÷ 6 =

l. 70 - 35 =

m. 10 × 8 =

n. 44 ÷ 11 =

o. 9 + 12 =

p. 12 + 16 =

q. 5 × 8 =

r. 80 - 25 =

8 What numbers should replace the question marks in order to have same value on both sides of equation?

a. 3 × 8 = 4 × ?

b. 5 + 15 = 10 × ?

c. 19 - 10 = 3 + ?

d. 27 - ? = 10 + 7

e. 12 ÷ ? = 15 - 11

f. 28 ÷ 4 = 18 - ?

g. ? ÷ 8 = 6 + 3

 9 What number replace the question marks to continue the sequence?

a. 1, 3, 5, 7, 9, ? ,...

b. 2, 4, 6, 8, 10, ? ,...

c. 1, 4, 7, 10, ? ,...

d. 10, 20, 30, 40, 50, ? ,...

e. 52, 54, 56, 58, 60, 62, ? ,...

f. 22, 33, 44, 55, 66, 77, 88, ? ,...

g. 25, 30, 35, 40, 45, 50, 55, ? ,...

h. 7, 14, 21, 28, 35, ? ,...

i. 9, 18, 27, 36, 45, ? ,...

Date   **Number of incorrect answers**   **Time duration**

Main weak points

Conclusion

Extra Exercises (Home-work)

1 Try to find all hidden items in the picture and circle them.

2 Try to find all hidden items in the picture and circle them.

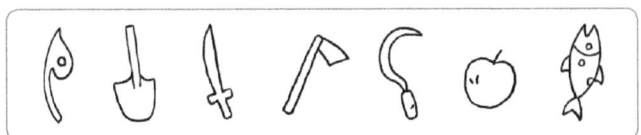

3 In this exercise, you can see different pictures of fruits labeled with a word. In some cases, the labeled word may be congruent with the picture, while in others they are incongruent. For the first part of the exercise, read just the words, but for the second part accurately name the pictures regardless of the written words underneath them. Record the time for both parts and compare them.

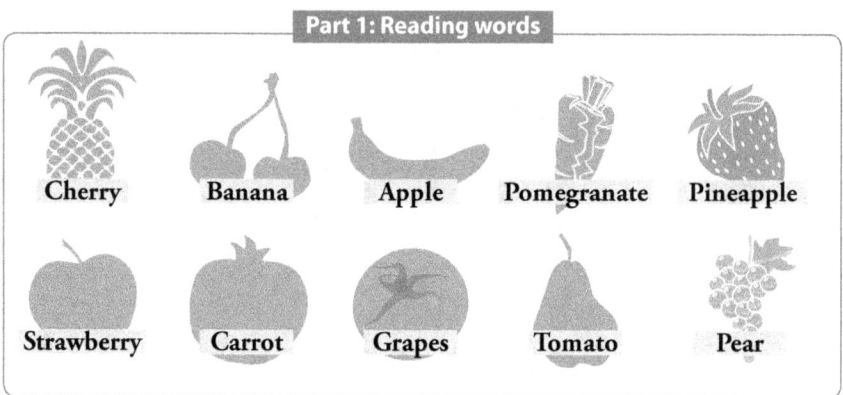

Time (sec): ....   Number of errors: ....

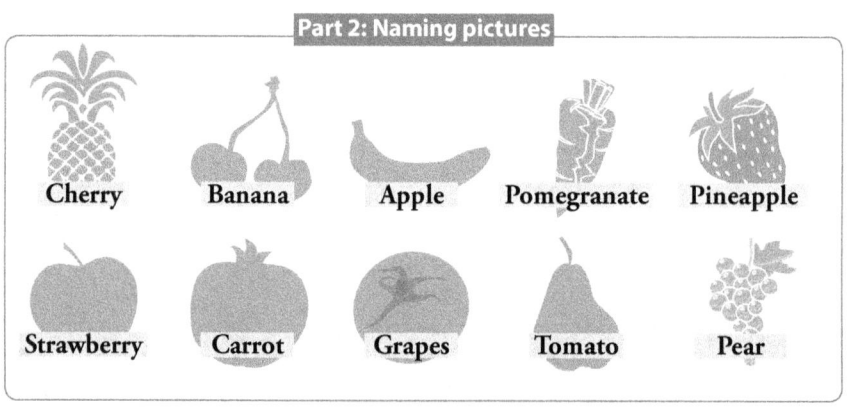

Time (sec): ....   Number of errors: ....

4 Look at the faces below and try to identify the emotion conveyed in each face.

 5 Scan the below image with your eyes and try to find as many as target pictures (images with same direction) without marking anything on the paper. Write the total number.

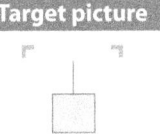

Total number: ....

6 Look carefully at the following three pairs of images and try to spot differences.

5 differences

5 differences

10 differences

 7 Calculate equations below and write the correct answers.

a. 47 - 5 =

b. 20 × 7 =

c. 28 ÷ 7 =

d. 13 × 2 =

e. 88 ÷ 11 =

f. 100 + 25 =

g. 55 - 12 =

h. 30 × 5 =

i. 11 + 73 =

j. 48 ÷ 2 =

k. 11 × 3 =

l. 10 + 18 =

m. 40 - 25 =

n. 66 ÷ 6 =

o. 7 × 9 =

p. 20 + 16 =

8 What numbers should replace the question marks in order to have same value on both sides of the equation?

a. 5 × 6 = 3 × ?

b. 7 + 8 = 5 × ?

c. 13 - 2 = 2 + ?

d. 42 - ? = 11 + 22

e. 32 ÷ ? = 19 - 11

f. 20 × 2 = 11 + ?

g. 2 + 16 = ? × 2

 9 What number replaces the question marks to continue the sequence?

a. 3, 6, 9, 12, 15, ? ,...

b. 24, 30, 36, 42, ? ,...

c. 1, 4, 9, 16, 25, ? ,...

d. 21, 28, 35, 42, 49, ? ,...

e. 35, 37, 39, 41, 43, 45, ? ,...

f. 66, 68, 70, 72, 74, ? ,...

g. 12, 14, 16, 18, 20, ? ,...

h. 4, 8, 12, 16, 20, ? ,...

i. 2, 6, 12, 20, 30, ? ,...

Date   Number of incorrect answers   Time duration

Main weak points

Conclusion

Brain Club
2nd Session

Brain Education

1 Is there any genetic susceptibility for incurring brain-function injuries from the use of Alcohol and other drugs?

As it has been shown in many studies, everyone has natural biological barriers that resist against the toxic effects caused by drugs in the body to some extent. Based on individual genetic structures, the strength of these barriers differ among people. Some people tend to resist these effects more than others and are influenced less by the adverse effect of drugs. But, we know that even among those who have a more resilient biological structure, the toxic effects of drugs are always more powerful than all the natural biological barriers.

2 Can a person experience different level of brain injuries, over time and in different situations from the same drug?

There is some limited evidence that suggests using drugs in different physiological and psychological states could influence the severity of resulted brain injuries. For example, using drugs when users experience a traumatic psychological or biological stress or fatigue or hunger could lead to more negative effects compared to once they experience non-stressed condition.

Brain Exercises (Main Session)

1 Read the below paragraphs and find the letters specified for each part.

A. Letter "D/d"

The health benefits of yogurt have always been important to mankind. Yogurt is a powerhouse of various vitamins and minerals that are also present in milk. Furthermore, yogurt is a good source of easily digestible proteins. Yogurt is beneficial for maintaining cholesterol levels in the body and preventing ailments like hypertension, while also boosting immunity. It is good for improving the strength of bones and teeth, aids in digestion, and is valuable in skin care.

Number of "D/d":

B. Letter "L/l"

The health benefits of fruits guarantee you optimum health and a well-built body in the long run. Fruits benefit your body immensely as they are natural sources of vitamins and minerals, which are essential for the proper functioning of the body. Rich in dietary fiber, fruits also help to improve the functioning of the digestive tract. Fruits are an important part of a healthy diet for those who want to lose weight; they give ample energy and nearly every nutrient that your body needs to curb weight gain, without adding any unnecessary fats.

Number of "L/l":

2 On this page, you see a series of numbers. Start from number 1 and draw a line to number 2, then to number 3, then to number 4 and so on until you reach to the last number, without lifting your pencil from the paper. You should draw the lines as fast as you can.

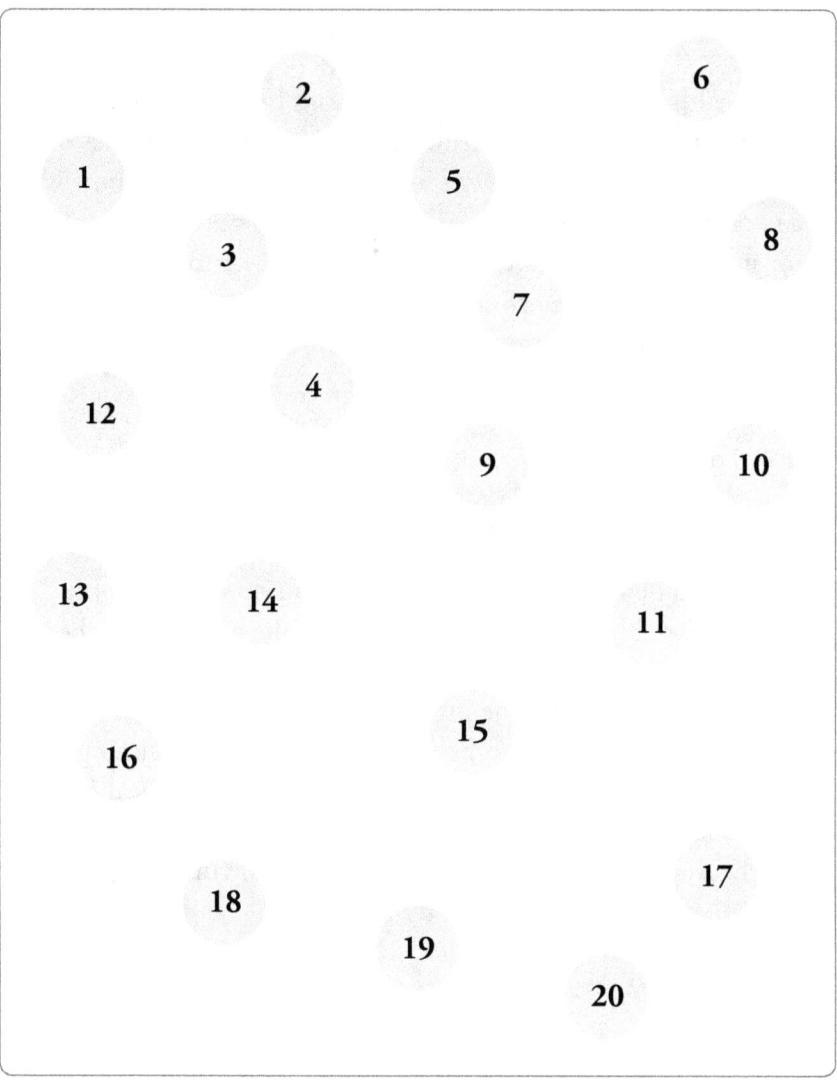

Time (sec): ....

3 Try to find a path between the gray and pink arrows that joins the entrance and the exit parts of the path.

4 See the figure below; then determine which three of the nine below figures are combined to form the main figure.

 5 Find the odd one in this series.

6 Which of the three tiles below completes the picture?

a.  b. 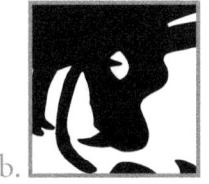 c.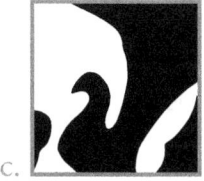

7 See the below picture and try to find all of the birds.

15 Birds

8 How many squares are in this picture?

Number of Squares:

 9 Read the numbers below and try to find all "3" and "8" numbers respectively and write the total numbers for each of them.

0	5	3	1	6	3	7	4	1	0	3	9	5	8	5	2	3	1
8	7	5	1	2	9	6	5	9	2	9	1	7	6	8	1	4	2
7	5	3	1	2	5	3	8	0	5	8	9	4	3	3	3	5	7
0	6	5	0	1	6	4	6	1	9	7	6	2	0	6	1	1	0
6	5	4	1	3	0	9	1	6	2	8	7	0	5	8	9	3	4
0	8	7	5	7	9	1	5	4	8	9	5	0	6	1	4	9	6
3	3	5	1	4	6	3	9	3	3	0	1	6	7	8	2	4	8
5	1	8	3	4	0	8	9	9	6	5	1	9	5	9	6	5	5
7	2	9	0	6	5	9	1	0	7	4	3	9	4	1	5	1	7

Number of "3":   **Number of "8":**

10 Among the hands below, find the right hands and the left hands.

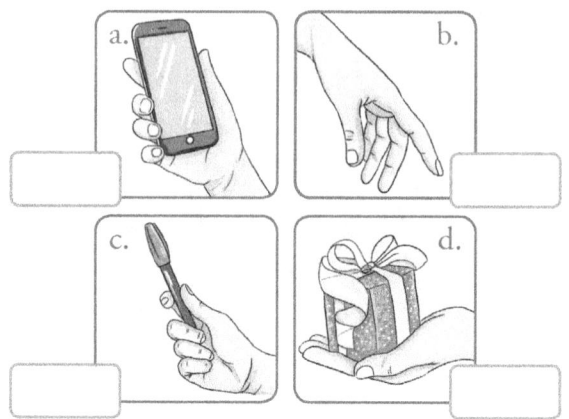

 11 Draw the other half of the picture.

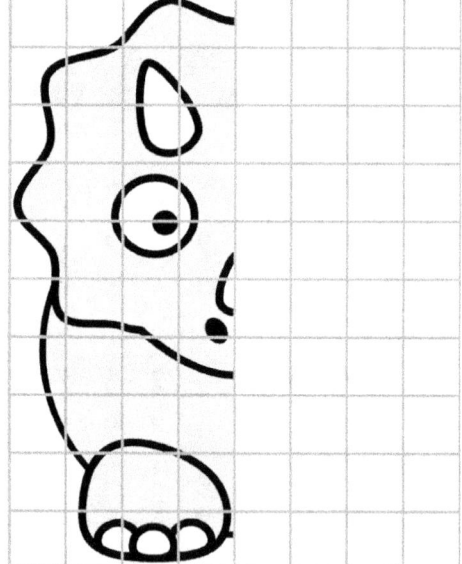

Report Card

Date   Number of incorrect answers   Time duration

Main weak points

Conclusion

Extra Exercises (Home-work)

1 Read the below paragraphs and find the letters specified for each part.

A. Letter "F/f"

Fitness is defined as the quality or state of being fit. Around 1950, perhaps consistent with the Industrial Revolution and the treatise of World War II, the term «fitness» increased in western vernacular by a factor of ten. Modern definition of fitness describes either a person or machines ability to perform a specific function or a holistic definition of human adaptability to cope with various situations. This has led to an interrelation of human fitness and attractiveness which has mobilized global fitness and fitness equipment industries. Regarding specific function, fitness is attributed to person who possesses significant aerobic or anaerobic ability, i.e. strength or endurance.

Number of "F/f":

B. Letter "C/c"

Health is the level of functional and metabolic efficiency of a living organism. In humans it is the ability of individuals or communities to adapt and self-manage when facing physical, mental, psychological and social changes. The World Health Organization (WHO) defined health in its broader sense in its 1948 constitution as «a state of complete physical, mental, and social well-being and not merely the absence of disease or infirmity." This definition has been subject to controversy, in particular as lacking operational value, the ambiguity in developing cohesive health strategies, and because of the problem created by use of the word «complete».

Number of "C/c":

2 On this page, you see a series of numbers. Start from number 1 and draw a line to number 2, then to number 3, then to number 4 and so on until you reach to the last number, without lifting your pencil from the paper. You should draw the lines as fast as you can.

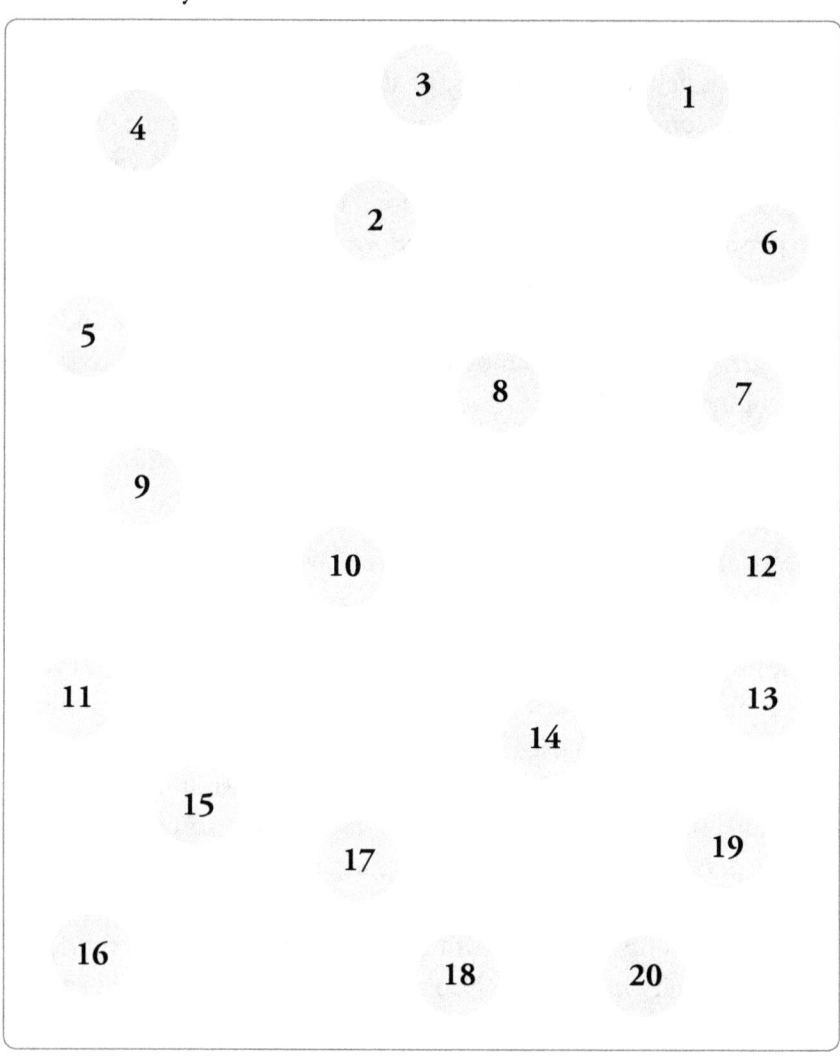

Time (sec):

3 Try to find a path between the gray and pink arrows that joins the entrance and exit parts of the path.

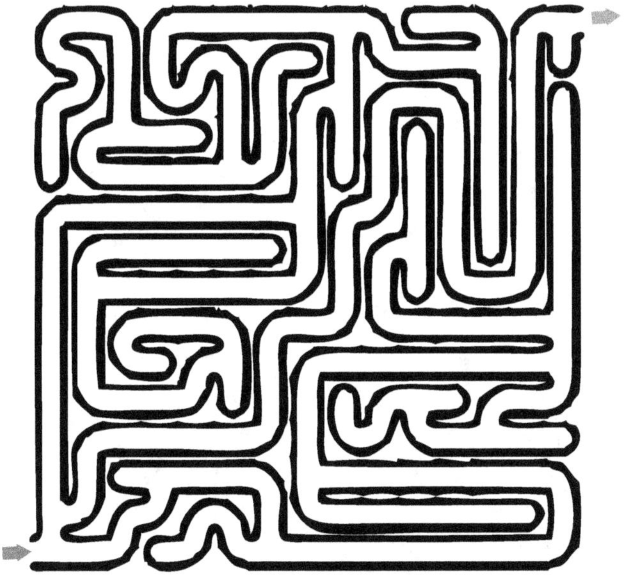

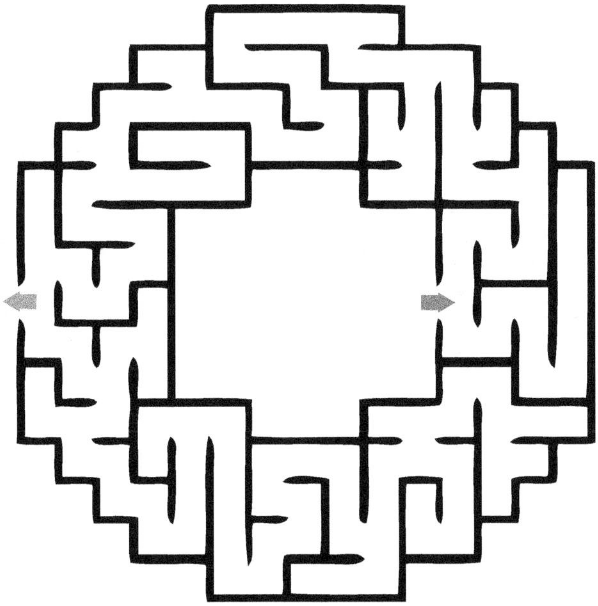

4 Which of the three tiles below completes the picture?

a.

b.

c.

5 How many squares are in this picture?

Number of Squares: ....

 6 Among the hands below, find the right hands and the left hands.

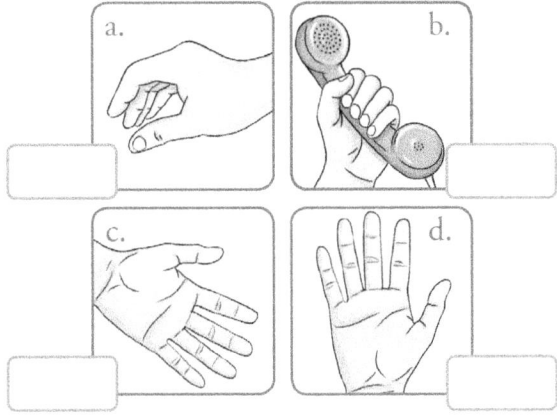

7 Which two of the six cropped tiles do not belong to the picture below?

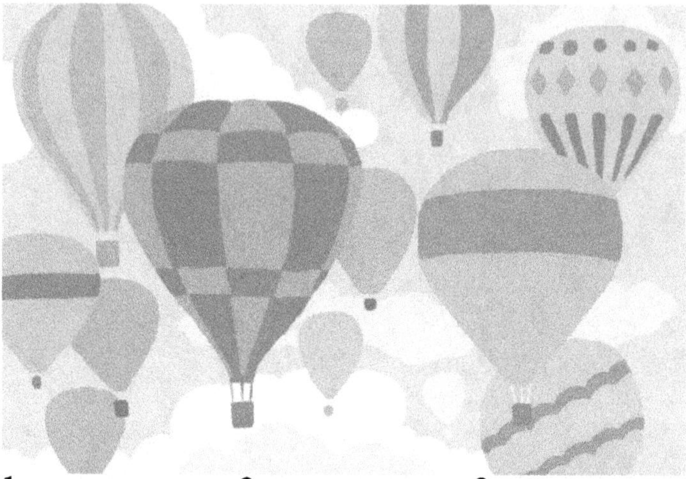

1.

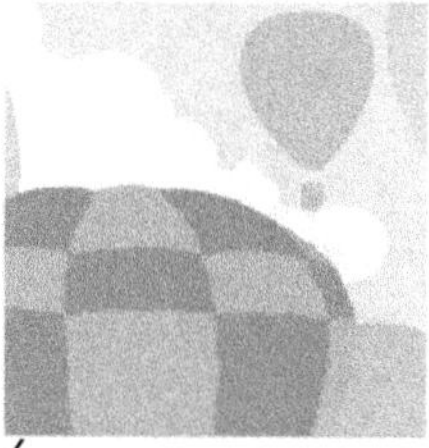

2.

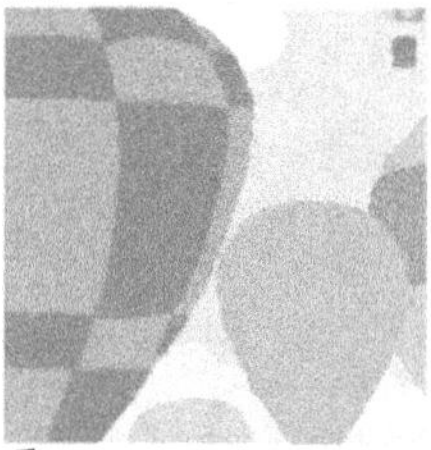

3.

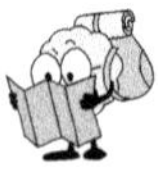

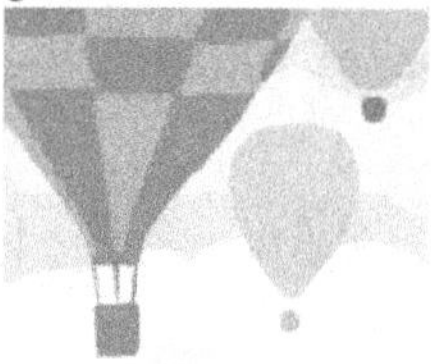

4.

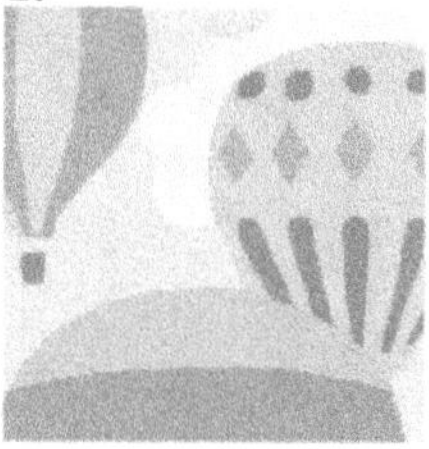

5.

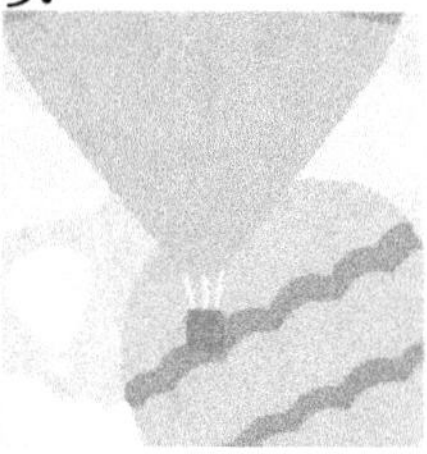

6.

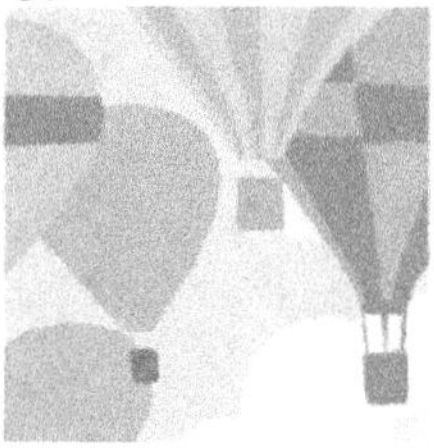

Report Card

Date **Number of incorrect answers** **Time duration**

Main weak points

Conclusion

Brain Club
3rd Session

Brain Education

1 Is there any way to prevent brain injuries during drug use?

Brain injuries are a natural result of alcohol and other drug use, but a positively altered lifestyle of users in abstinence prove to be effective in decreasing the severity of these injuries. As we will address in part 2, there are some useful "to do" lists that could help users in this way. For example, a healthy diet with antioxidant foods, sufficient sleep, peaceful/less stressful environments and healthy social connections could be effective in alleviating the toxic effects and harm caused by drugs, conditions that are not usually associated with drug use.

2 How can I recognize my own level of brain-function injury?

As you become more mindful of you brain's functions, your first-hand knowledge, when you begin to feel and recognize effects of your level of brain injuries will alert you to the symptoms of your brain dysfunctions. In the first part of the book, we have summarized the 10 most important signs/symptoms that you can note in your daily life activities. You may also monitor changes of these injuries in terms of their severity over time, with your careful introspection. But, introspection and insight, as important brain functions, can also be affected with drug use. Therefore, many drug users do not realize the adverse effects of drugs on their brain for a long time. A few weeks of abstinence often help people to recover a minimum level of introspection and insight to be able to recognize their brain injuries. This is the time that we believe your use of this book will be helpful.

Brain Exercises (Main Session)

 1 Try to remember one memorable event occurred on the specified days.

Yesterday: ....

Same day last week: ....

2 Mark the right answer.

The relation between "going" and "coming" is the same as "arriving" and...
a. Bus ☐ b. Running ☐
c. Airplane ☐ d. Leaving ☐

The relation between "left" and "right" is the same as "below" and...
a. Roof ☐ b. Ground ☐
c. Above ☐ d. Under ☐

The relation between "rose" and "flower" is the same as "dog" and...
a. Cat ☐ b. Human ☐
c. Bird ☐ d. Animal ☐

The relation between "pen" and "pencil" is the same as "bookcase" and...
a. Sofa ☐ b. Book ☐
c. Closet ☐ d. Paper ☐

3 Look at the below picture for 5 seconds and then turn to the next page.

Without returning to the previous page, try to find the similar picture as you have seen on previous page.

a.
b.
c.
d.
e.
f.

4 Take a careful look at these two sets of characters. Which characters appear in the series on the right but not in the series on the left?

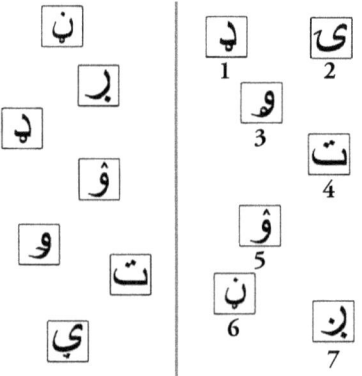

5 Find the odd word in each series.

a. Car ☐ Bus ☐ Train ☐ Truck ☐ ☐
b. Apple ☐ Carrot ☐ Cabbage ☐ Spinach ☐ ☐
c. Telephone ☐ Fax ☐ Cellphone ☐ Camera ☐ ☐

 6 Try to find the logical order of the below pictures.

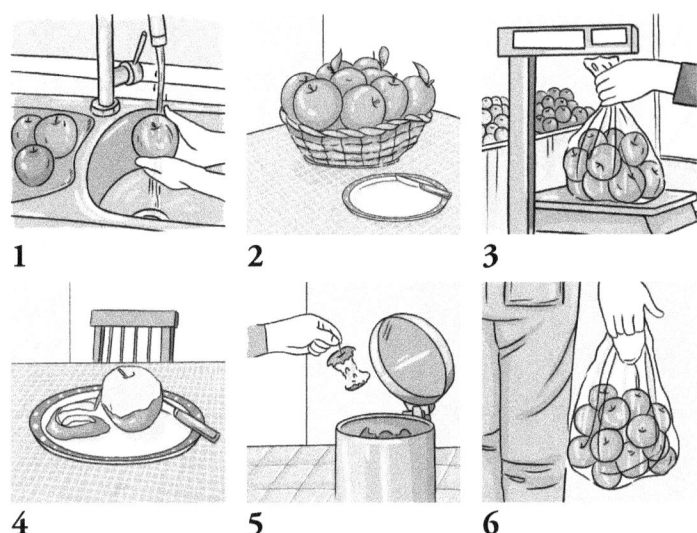

1 2 3

4 5 6

The right sequence of pictures (from left to right): ....

 7 Look at the below picture for 10 seconds and then turn to the next page.

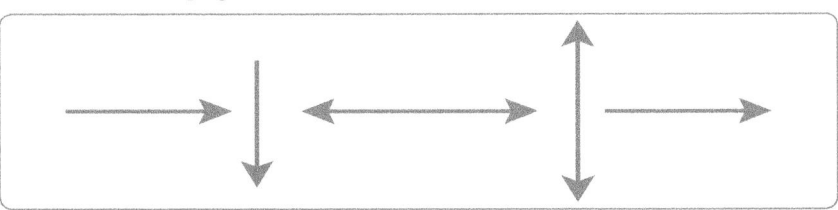

Without returning to the previous page, try to find the similar picture as you have seen on previous page.

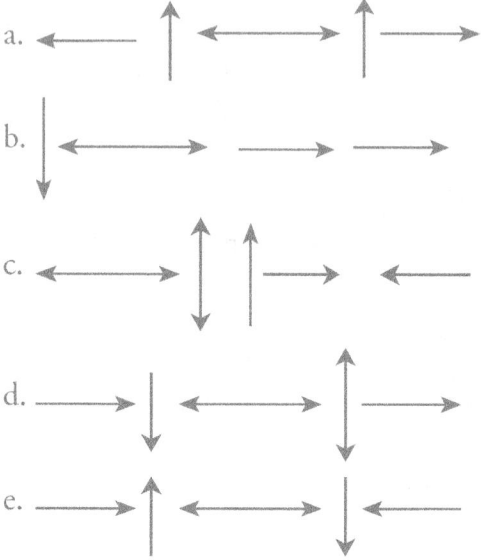

8 Write a paragraph with the name of below images and use each of them only once.

....
....
....

9 Find the right connection between brands and products.

Cellphone	○	○ McDonalds
Watch	○	○ Nike
Jeans	○	○ Apple
Sportswear	○	○ Starbucks
Burger	○	○ Levi's
Coffee	○	○ Swatch

 10 Look at the below pictures for 25 seconds and then turn to the next page.

Without returning to the previous page, try to recall as many pictures as you can.

....

....

....

....

 11 Try to solve the below Sudoku puzzle. Note that each row, column, and nonet (sections of nine borderd cells) must contain each number (typically 1 to 9) just once.

4	3	6		7		2	5	9
5	7		2	9	6	1	4	
	2	1		4	5			8
6		3	4	8	1	7	2	
7	1		5		9	3	8	4
	4	5		2			1	6
1	8	9		5		4	3	2
2	6		8		4			1
3		4	9	1		8	6	7

 12 Look at the below pictures for 5 seconds and then turn to the next page.

Without turning to the previous page, try to redraw four the types of weather images on the blank clouds as precisely as possible.

13 Try to find the names of determined fruits in the below cross-word table.

R	A	W	A	Y	R	Y	A	Y	A	P	A	P	B
B	N	E	E	R	L	R	A	B	B	Y	E	E	L
N	A	E	B	R	M	R	N	E	A	R	W	A	U
B	N	S	A	E	P	E	R	N	N	R	A	I	E
R	A	A	P	B	E	B	E	P	E	E	T	B	B
S	B	L	B	K	E	P	O	E	A	B	E	N	E
E	S	I	R	C	A	S	A	P	T	W	R	K	R
E	Y	B	I	A	Y	A	E	E	E	A	M	L	R
G	E	R	W	L	O	R	E	P	N	R	E	Y	Y
N	P	R	I	B	B	N	M	L	T	T	L	M	M
A	A	A	K	C	O	R	E	R	L	S	O	O	N
R	R	A	R	M	A	E	L	I	M	E	N	E	C
O	G	S	E	G	N	M	P	E	B	R	K	I	T
S	P	L	A	E	E	L	P	P	A	B	E	W	I

RASPBERRY
LIME
BLACKBERRY
BLUEBERRY
WATERMELON
ORANGE
PAPAYA
KIWI
STRAWBERRY
GRAPE
APPLE

Date   **Number of incorrect answers**   **Time duration**
Main weak points

Conclusion

Report Card

Extra Exercises (Home-work)

1 Try to name as many as things that are naturally created in green and white colors in just 60 seconds. See the examples.

Green: for example : grass
White: for example: snow

2 Mark the right answer

The relation between "planet" and "star" is the same as "bird" and...

a. Reptile ☐   b. Crow ☐
c. Zoo ☐   d. Cat ☐

The relation between "ear" and "hearing" is the same as "eye" and...

a. Face ☐   b. Seeing ☐
c. Laughing ☐   d. Sleeping ☐

The relation between "hand" and "clock" is the same as "wheel" and...

a. Car ☐   b. Driving ☐
c. Break ☐   d. Downhill ☐

The relation between "eating" and "drinking" is the same as "running" and...

a. Cycling ☐   b. Studying ☐
c. Sleeping ☐   d. Talking ☐

3 Look at the below pictures and numbers for 10 seconds and then turn to the next page.

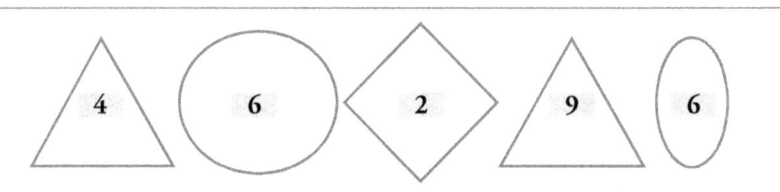

a. Which pictures have been repeated two times in the series? write their numbers.

b. Which numbers have been repeated two times in the series? write their numbers.

4 Take a careful look at these two sets of characters. Which characters appear in the series on the right but not in the series on the left?

5 Find the odd words in each series.

a. Piano ☐ Dulcimer ☐ Flute ☐ Daf ☐
b. Triangle ☐ Oval ☐ Square ☐ Diamond ☐
c. Refrigerator ☐ Cabinet ☐ Washing machine ☐ Fan ☐

3rd step | 51

6 Try to find the logical order of the below pictures.

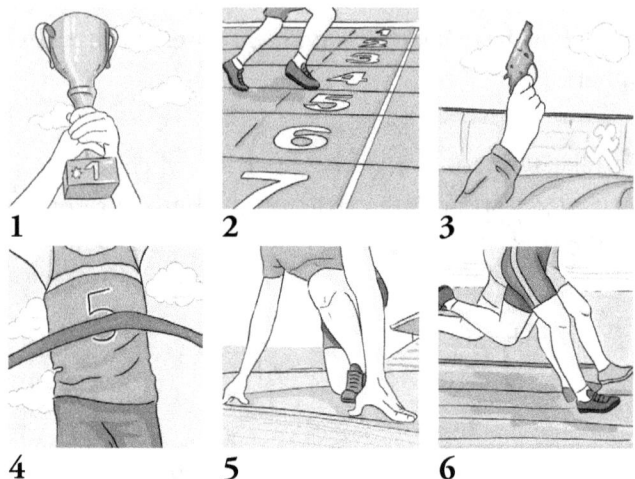

The right sequence of pictures (from left to right): ....

 7 Write a paragraph with the below words and use each of them only once.

strawberry, school, television, ice-cream, girl, bicycle, afternoon

....
....
....

 8 Look at the below pictures for 10 seconds and then turn to the next page.

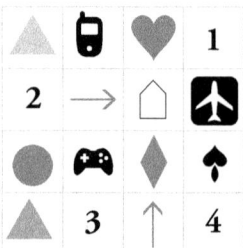

52 | Brain Club

Without turning to the previous page, answer these questions:

a. **Compared to the picture you have seen in previous page, which two numbers have changed places?**

b. **Compared to the picture you have seen in previous page, which two symbols have changed their places?**

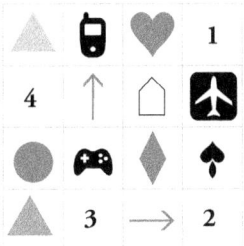

9 Try to solve the Sudoku puzzle below. Note that each row, column, and nonet (sections of nine bordered cells) must contain each number (typically 1 to 9) just once.

4		7		5	1		6	2
9		5	4	2		7		3
2	3	6		8	9	5		1
3		4		1	5	6	2	
1		2	9		4		5	8
5	7	8	2			1		4
		3	1	9	8		7	5
7	5			4		3		
8	2			3	7	4	1	6

3rd step | 53

10 Try to complete the below cross-word.

Across
1. Firm hold
3. Prepare present
6. Vatican leader
9. Hand over, for a price
11. Hand a seat
12. Midmonth day
13. A great distance
14. Target towards a goal
15. Seek divine guidance
17. Hunter's quarry
20. More than want
21. Catch sight of

Down
1. Space between 2 things
2. Little rascal
4. Be remorseful
5. Chum
7. Demand
8. Written report
9. Official seal
10. Skedaddle
15. Bit of wordplay
16. Chopping tool
18. Tide type
19. So far

11 Try to briefly summarize the last movie you have seen.

....
....
....

 12 Look at the below picture for 20 seconds and then turn to the next page.

Without turning to the previous page answer these questions:

A. How many people were in the picture?

a. 4 people ☐
b. 5 people ☐
c. 6 people ☐

B. Which animal you saw in the picture?

a. Cat ☐
b. Dog ☐
c. Rabbit ☐

C. Which one was on the floor?

a. Dish ☐
b. Toy ☐
c. Book ☐

D. What were children eating?

a. Fruit ☐
b. Ice-cream ☐
c. Tea ☐

Report Card

Date   **Number of incorrect answers**   **Time duration**

Main weak points

Conclusion

Brain Club
4th Session

Brain Education

1 What is the effect of overdose on my brain functions?

Overdose is one of the worst parts of drug use due to its mechanism. Each time users experience overdose, a large amount of toxic substances enter the body to the degree that our natural bodily functions cannot neutralize and fully eliminate these toxins. Furthermore, during overdose with some drugs like opioids, drug users may experience respiratory depression and apnea which may lead to insufficient flow of oxygen to different body organs, especially in the brain, that leads to more severe injuries.

2 What is the effect of chronic relapse on to my brain functions?

We all have natural biological barriers that protect and defend our brain and body against foreign substances and toxins. These barriers become more active during drug use in response to frequent exposures to the drug toxins trying to overcome a part of their negative effects. These natural barriers decrease their activities in the absence of toxins after a few weeks of abstinence. So, each time a user returns to drugs after a period of abstinence, as the resisting power of these barriers is reduced, more toxic substances pass through them and reach different parts of the brain. Numerous relapse prevention interventions and techniques, including mindfulness exercises, help us to diminish this effect by reducing the number of relapses during the process of recovery.

Brain Exercises (Main Session)

 1 Try to find all hidden items in the picture and circle them.

2 Try to find all hidden items in the picture and circle them.

3 In this exercise, you can see different pictures of geometric shapes labeled with a word. In some cases, the labeled word may be congruent with the shape, while in some others they are incongruent. For the first part of exercise, read just the words, but for the second part accurately name shapes regardless of the written words. Record your time for both parts and compare them.

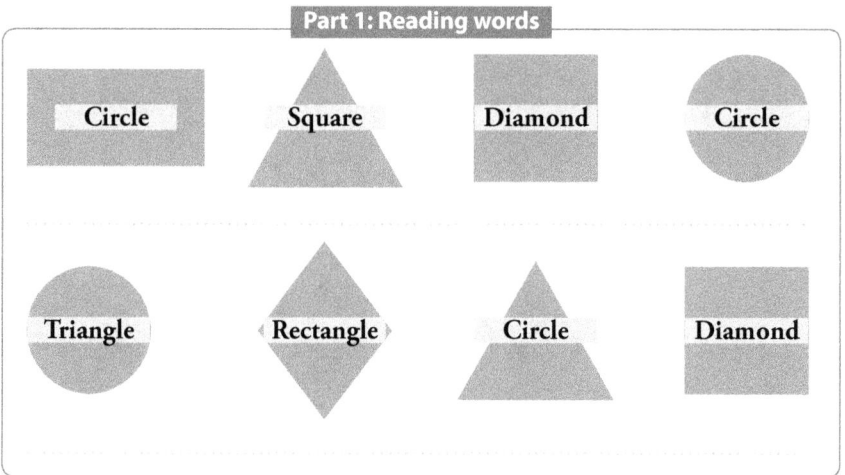

Time (sec): .... Number of errors: ....

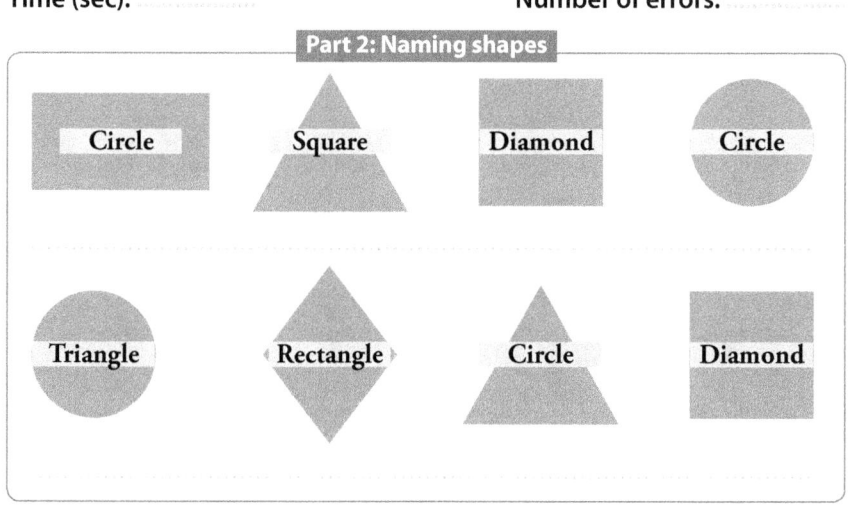

Time (sec): .... Number of errors: ....

4 Scan the below images and try to find as many as target pictures and mark them as identified for each target picture. Write the total number.

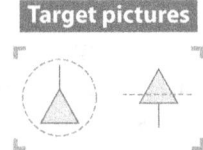

Total number : .... △

Total number: .... ⚊△⚊

5 Look carefully at the following two pairs of images and try to spot differences.

13 differences

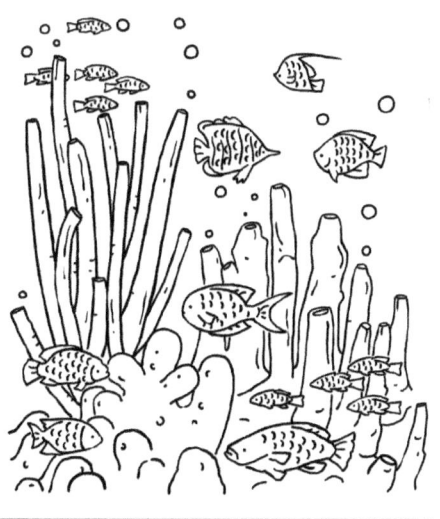

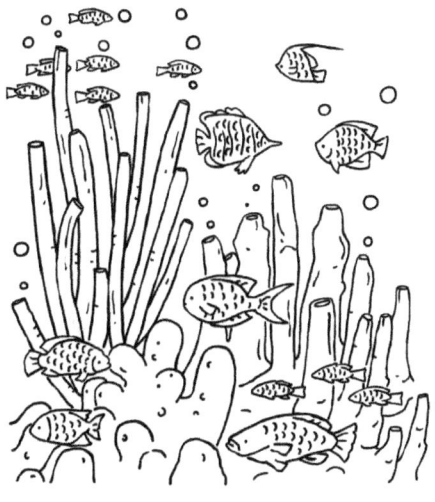

8 differences

 6 Calculate equations below and write the answers.

a. 64 + 13 =

b. 250 ÷ 5 =

c. 53 - 27 =

d. 71 × 6 =

e. 224 ÷ 4 =

f. 17 + 59 =

g. 8 + 60 =

h. 120 - 40 =

i. 60 + 16 =

j. 41 + 22 =

k. 78 - 19 =

l. 86 - 16 =

m. 14 × 3 =

n. 22 × 9 =

7 What numbers should replace the question marks in order to have same value on both sides of equation?

a. 10 × 5 = ? × ?

b. 20 + 16 = 12 × ?

c. 81 - 9 = 3 + ?

d. 225 + 5 = ? × ?

e. 48 - 8 = ? + ?

f. 100 - 12 = ? × ?

g. 17 + ? = 9 × 7

8 What number replace the question marks to continue the sequence?

a. 2, 3, 5, 8, 13, 21, ?

b. 114, 118, 122, 126, ?

c. 2, 5, 10, 50, 500, 25000, ?

d. 1, 8, 27, 64, 125, ?

e. 9, 18, 27, 36, 45, ?

f. 100, 81, 64, 49, 36, ?

g. 71, 73, 75, 77, 79, ?

h. 6, 11, 16, 21, ?

Date   Number of incorrect answers   Time duration

Main weak points

Conclusion

Report Card

⚡ Extra Exercises (Home-work)

 1 In this exercise, you can see different pictures of geometric shapes labeled with a word. In some cases, the labeled word may be congruent with the shape, while in some others they are incongruent. For the first part of exercise, read just the words, but for the second part accurately name shapes regardless of the written words. Record your time for both parts and compare them.

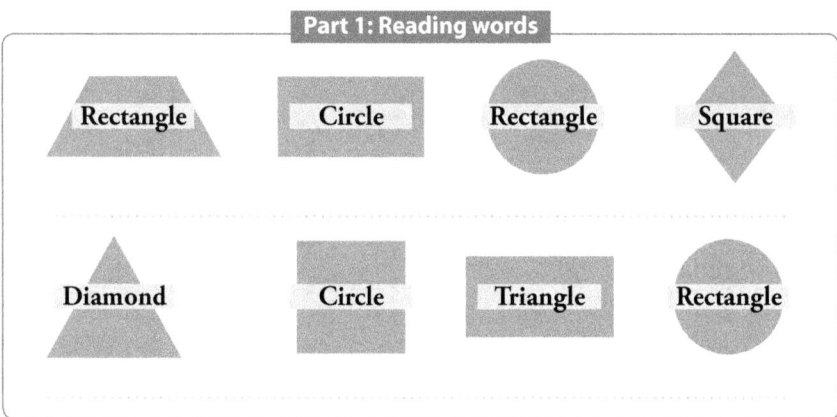

Time (sec): .... **Number of errors:** ....

Time (sec): .... **Number of errors:** ....

2 Try to find the specified items in the picture and circle them.

3 mice

3 Try to find all hidden items in the picture and circle them.

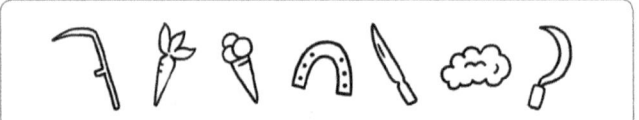

4 Look at the faces below and try to identify the emotion conveyed in each face.

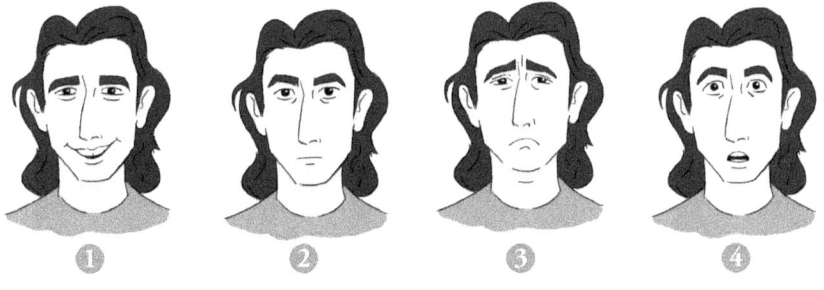

5 Scan the below images and try to find as many as target pictures and mark them as identified for each target picture. Write the total number.

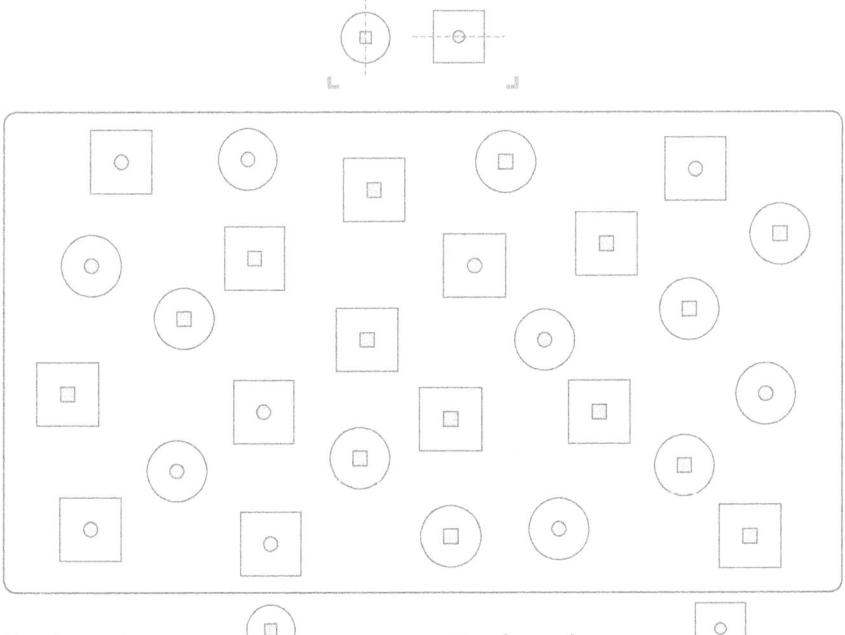

Total number: .... **Total number:** ....

6 Look carefully at the next two pairs of images below and try to spot differences.

9 differences

8 differences

 **7** Answer the below questions.

a. The sum of even numbers: 4, 7, 1, 8, 3, 6, 9, 2, 8, 4
b. The sum of odd numbers: 3, 6, 4, 4, 9, 6, 7, 5, 8, 1, 3
c. Even numbers multiplication: 3, 2, 1, 6, 4, 2, 7, 4, 9, 8
d. Odd number multiplication: 4 , 3 , 3 , 2 , 7 , 2 , 2 , 9 , 1 , 1 , 6
e. What number should replace the question mark?
10, 10, 11, 13, 16, ?
100, 96, 92, 88, 84, ?
f. Multiply 2 × 1242
g. Calculate the mean (add up all the numbers, then divide by how many numbers there are) of numbers in each series.
1, 4, 5, 1,4, 2, 11:
1, 2, 1, 3, 8, 3:

8 What numbers should replace the question marks?

a. 23 × 42 = 9 ? 6
b. 15 × 13 = ? 9 5

9 What numbers should replace the question marks?

a.

2	5	1	3	6	2		5	3	6	2	4	2
3	7	4	7	11	8		6	5	?	?	?	?

b.

5	4	7	8	6	3		7	9	8	2	5	3
10	2	14	4	3	6		14	4/5	?	?	?	?

Report Card

Date   **Number of incorrect answers**   **Time duration**
Main weak points

Conclusion

Brain Club
5th Session

⚡ Brain Education

1 What areas/functions in the brain heal slowest/fastest?

Some parts of brain can heal faster than others. For example, it has been found that attention and working memory may improve at the early stage of abstinence and brain training, though other complicated functions such as decision making and planning may need more time and training to improve in the process of recovery.

2 Can I recapture (or improve) all my brain power during recovery?

Although using drugs especially after a long and intensive using episode could lead to sever brain injuries, but there is a real hope in restoring major parts of these injuries over time. Recent studies in this field show that there are some exercises and techniques that could help users to achieve their brain power during recovery period. You can find 10 of the most 10 practical strategies, exercises and guides in the following parts of this book.

Brain Exercises (Main Session)

 1 Read the below paragraphs and find the letters specified for each part.

A. Letter "P/p"

The red blood cells of mammals are typically shaped as biconcave disks: flattened and depressed in the center, with a dumbbell-shaped cross section, and a torus-shaped rim on the edge of the disk. This distinctive biconcave shape optimizes the flow properties of blood in the large vessels, such as maximization of laminar flow and minimization of platelet scatter, which suppresses their atherogenic activity in those large vessels. However, there are some exceptions concerning shape in the artiodactyl order (even-toed ungulates including cattle, deer, and their relatives), which displays a wide variety of bizarre red blood cell morphologies: small and highly ovaloid cells in llamas and camels, tiny spherical cells in mouse deer, and cells which assume fusiform, lanceolate, crescentic, and irregularly polygonal and other angular forms in red deer and wapiti. Members of this order have clearly evolved a mode of red blood cell development substantially different from the mammalian norm. Overall, mammalian red blood cells are remarkably flexible and deformable so as to squeeze through tiny capillaries, as well as to maximize their apposing surface by assuming a cigar shape, where they efficiently release their oxygen load.

Number of letter "P/p":

B. Letter "H/h"

The health benefits of apple include improved digestion, prevention of stomach disorders, gallstones, constipation, liver disorders, anemia, diabetes, heart disease, rheumatism, eye disorders, a variety of cancers, and gout. It also helps in improving weakness and provides relief from dysentery. Apples also help in treating dysentery. Furthermore, they can prevent the onset of Alzheimer's and Parkinson's disease. Finally, they aid in dental care and skin care. Apples are some of the most popular and delicious fruits on the planet, and there is nothing like biting into a bright, red, juicy apple to quench your thirst and satisfy your sweet tooth, all while boosting your health in a major way. The skin of apples is thin, but sturdy, and the inner flesh is thick and juicy, and it softens as it ripens. The inner core holds the seeds, which are hard and difficult to digest. The nutrients are in the flesh and the skin, which is a rich source of various tannins that give its color.

Number of letter "H/h":

2 Link the 12 squares on this page without raising your pencil. You cannot touch circles, and you cannot pass through each square more than once!

Time (sec):

3 Try to find a path between the gray and pink arrows that joins the entrance and the exit parts of the path.

4 Try to find letters "M" and "N" simultaneously and mark them.

M	O	L	T	T	N	M	T	M
L	O	T	N	M	L	O	M	L
N	T	L	O	O	M	T	L	O
M	L	M	N	T	O	N	M	T
O	N	O	T	O	N	M	T	L
T	M	L	O	T	M	L	N	M
N	O	N	M	M	O	T	O	N
M	N	L	O	N	T	L	M	L
O	L	N	L	T	M	O	T	N
L	O	T	M	O	O	T	L	T
N	T	M	N	L	N	T	N	O
N	O	L	M	T	O	N	O	M
T	M	O	N	M	T	M	N	T
N	L	T	O	L	O	L	M	O
M	T	L	N	O	M	T	O	L

Number of letter "M": ....
Number of letter "N": ....

 5 Look at the below picture. One tile is missing. Select the missing piece.

a.

b.

c.

6 Find the odd one in this series.

```
x x x x x x x x x x x x x x x x x x x x x x x x x x
x x x x x x x x x x x x x x x x x x x x x x x x x x
x x x x x x x x x x x x x x x x x x x x x x x x x x
x x x x x x x x x x x x x x x x x x x x x x x x x x
x x x x x x x x x x x x x x x x x x x x x x x x x x
x x x x x x x x x x x x x x x x x x x x x x x x x x
```

```
e' e' e' e' e' e' e' e' e' e' e' e' e' e' e' e' e' e' e'
e' e' e' e' e' e' e' e' e' e' e' e' e' e' e' e' e' e' e'
e' e' e' e' e' e' e' 'e e' e' e' e' e' e' e' e' e' e' e'
e' e' e' e' e' e' e' e' e' e' e' e' e' e' e' e' e' e' e'
e' e' e' e' e' e' e' e' e' e' e' e' e' e' e' e' e' e' e'
e' e' e' e' e' e' e' e' e' e' e' e' e' e' e' e' e' e' e'
```

 7 which two of the nine pictures are exactly the same?

8 To reach the point where the triangle is located, how many right and left turns must you make from the circle?

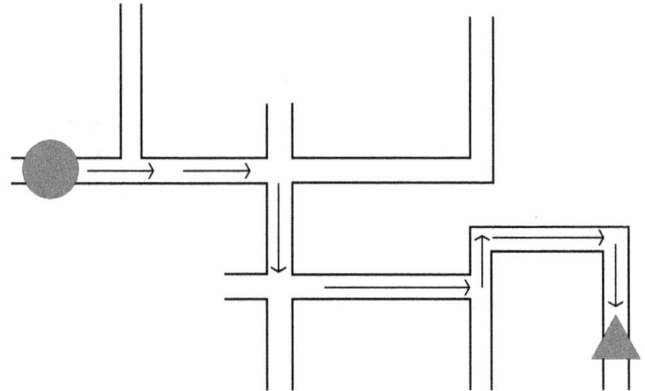

Number of turns to the left: ....
Number of turns to the right: ....

 9 How many triangles are in this picture?

Number of triangles: ....

Report Card

Date   **Number of incorrect answers**   **Time duration**
Main weak points

Conclusion

Extra Exercises (Home-work)

 1 Read the below paragraphs and find the letter determined for each part.

A. Letter "S/s"

Health benefits of white tea include reduced risk of cancer, cardiovascular disorder and improvement in oral health. It has antioxidant and anti-aging properties which help in maintaining good health and healthy skin. It protects skin from the harmful effects of UV light. With its antibacterial properties white tea protects the body from various infection causing bacteria. White tea provides relief to diabetic people from symptoms such as decrease plasma glucose levels, increase insulin secretion and excessive thirst. Intake of white tea also helps in losing weight. Though white tea is consumed as a common beverage, it has plenty of health benefits that can be accounted for after several studies have been carried out both in the present and in the past as well. Due to these benefits it is considered as a better alternative than coffee which contains high percentage of caffeine.

Number of letter "S/s":

B. Letter "E/e"

Emotion is any relatively brief conscious experience characterized by intense mental activity and a high degree of pleasure or displeasure. Scientific discourse has drifted to other meanings and there is no consensus on a definition. Emotion is often intertwined with mood, temperament, personality, disposition, and motivation. In some theories, cognition is an important aspect of emotion. Those acting primarily on the emotions they are feeling may seem as if they are not thinking, but mental processes are still essential, particularly in the interpretation of events. For example, the realization of our believing that we are in a dangerous situation and the subsequent arousal of our body›s nervous system is integral to the experience of our feeling afraid. Other theories, however, claim that emotion is separate from and can precede cognition. Emotions are complex. According to some theories, they are states of feeling that result in physical and psychological changes that influence our behavior. The physiology of emotion is closely linked to arousal of the nervous system with various states and strengths of arousal relating, apparently, to particular emotions.

Number of letter "E/e":

2 Link the 12 roses on this page without raising your pencil. You cannot touch leaves, and you cannot pass through each rose more than once!

Time (sec):

3 Read the below numbers and try to find both numbers "4" and "7" simultaneously.

8	3	7	6	1	5	7	5	7	2	6	9	5	4	8	7	2	1
7	1	0	6	5	9	8	1	6	2	1	5	5	9	1	4	3	9
1	9	3	1	6	4	3	3	8	4	2	6	0	1	0	6	5	8
2	2	0	9	4	0	0	1	2	8	2	1	2	1	7	0	6	9
1	8	5	2	2	9	8	4	6	1	4	0	1	8	6	2	6	2
6	2	2	5	7	3	3	3	7	6	6	6	9	3	2	8	2	4
0	7	5	3	5	4	3	7	7	6	5	8	6	5	2	0	4	1
1	7	9	4	6	4	0	9	3	3	9	2	4	3	3	7	8	3
0	1	8	3	2	1	8	6	2	8	7	0	3	9	6	2	2	6
2	7	3	8	2	6	6	7	1	9	8	8	9	2	6	1	0	3
6	0	6	9	9	6	7	4	8	3	1	8	4	9	2	2	7	4
3	3	7	4	6	1	6	8	5	7	9	9	6	5	2	2	2	3
7	9	1	0	8	5	3	5	9	2	5	8	5	0	1	9	4	0
6	0	5	3	7	4	9	0	5	3	5	9	0	1	0	9	0	1
4	8	5	1	7	8	3	8	2	2	7	7	2	9	0	9	3	8
3	7	6	4	9	1	9	1	3	6	6	6	4	5	6	4	0	6
6	2	7	3	9	6	7	5	9	3	8	9	6	2	1	6	5	3
8	3	9	1	3	3	1	0	2	9	2	0	0	1	8	1	1	7
1	0	9	6	3	8	3	2	9	8	7	3	6	1	5	6	5	3
0	1	6	5	0	2	9	4	7	8	6	3	6	0	4	3	7	5
3	7	4	2	6	1	9	7	0	1	3	9	6	8	7	3	4	1
3	4	0	3	6	7	1	2	7	2	5	5	1	7	8	0	8	0
6	9	7	4	7	6	0	2	7	1	5	0	2	4	2	9	2	8
0	2	6	5	6	0	1	5	5	1	9	0	3	8	8	7	2	3
2	1	0	3	8	4	7	0	0	1	8	9	3	6	4	3	2	1
1	8	2	9	8	1	7	5	1	6	3	6	3	3	9	2	7	0
2	6	4	7	5	3	8	7	4	9	7	6	5	1	9	6	3	5
2	0	9	1	0	3	7	5	1	0	2	8	1	6	3	0	4	1

Number of "4": .... Number of "7": ....

4 Try to find a path between the gray and pink arrows that joins the entrance and the exit parts of the path.

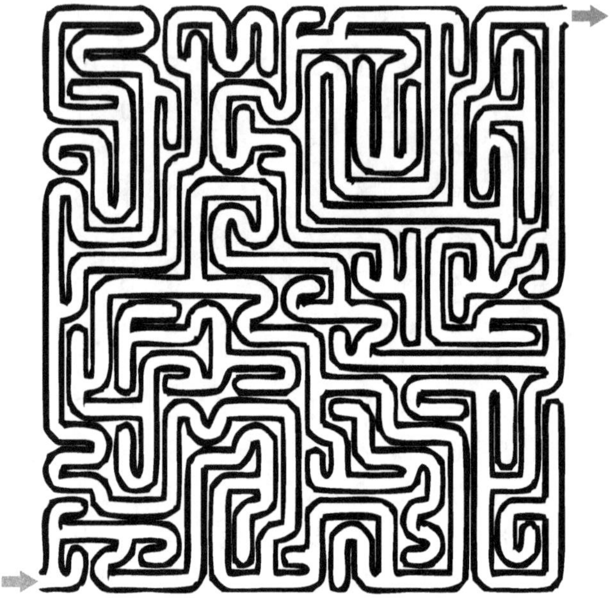

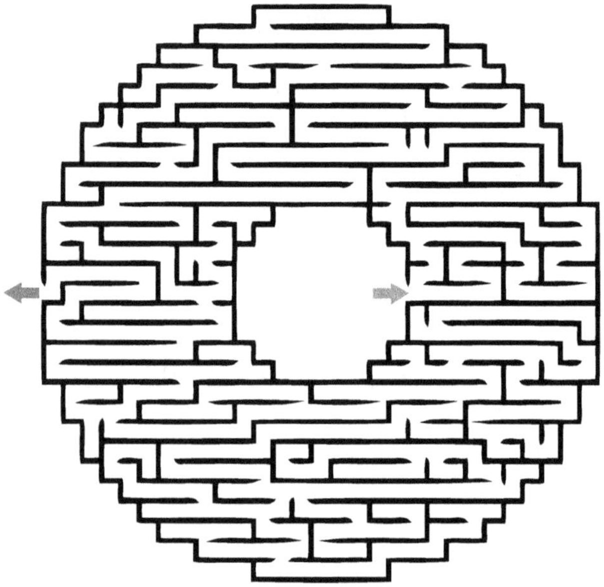

5 Which two of the nine pictures are exactly the same?

 6 Find the odd one in this series.

hhhhhhhhhhhhhhhhhhhhhhhhhhhhhhhhhh
hhhhhhhhhhhhhhhhhhhhhhhhhhhhhhhhhh
hhhhhhhhnhhhhhhhhhhhhhhhhhhhhhhhhh
hhhhhhhhhhhhhhhhhhhhhhhhhhhhhhhhhh
hhhhhhhhhhhhhhhhhhhhhhhhhhhhhhhhhh
hhhhhhhhhhhhhhhhhhhhhhhhhhhhhhhhhh

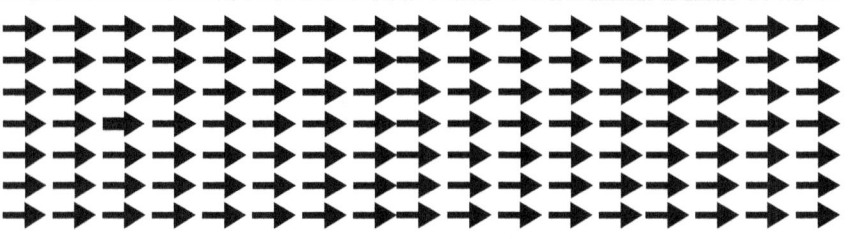

7 See the figure below; then determine which three of the nine below figures are combined to form the main figure?

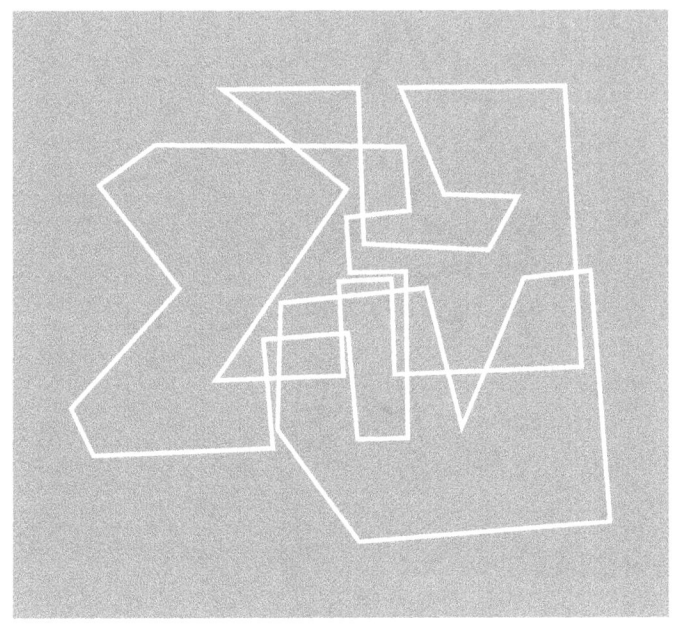

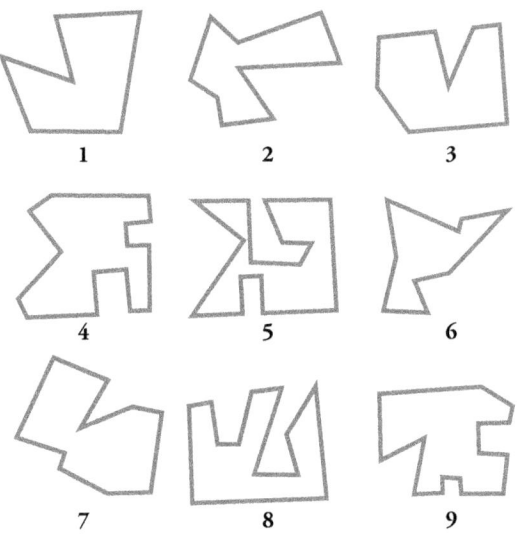

8 How many stars and triangles are in this picture?

Number of stars: ....
Number of triangles: ....

 9 Among the hands below, find the right hands and the left hands

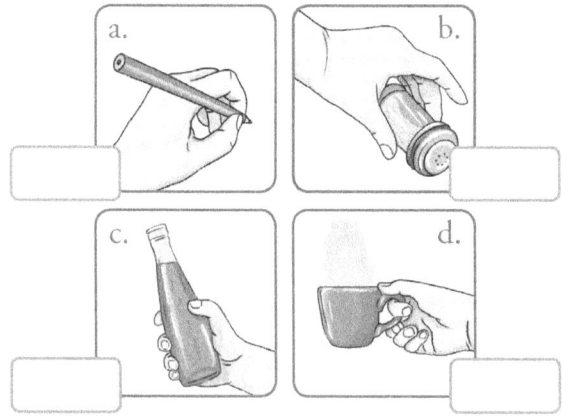

Report Card

Date **Number of incorrect answers** **Time duration**
Main weak points

Conclusion

Brain Club
6th Session

 **Brain Education**

1 Can I regain my brain's lost abilities?

Although using drugs for a long time could lead to damage is various brain areas, thus reducing brain functions, the good news is that our brain is mendable because of a fascinating feature called neuroplasticity. Due to this ability, our brain can repair itself in some degrees and gradually renew its functional power. So, during the term of abstinence, your brain can reorganize its structure without the presence of drugs and little-by-little restore its functions. Meanwhile, there are ways to boost this recovery process.

2 How much time does it take to get back my Brain's Power?

Your damaged brain is similar to a broken arm. As much as the broken arm needs to rest in a cast without movement, your brain needs a good time after detoxification phase to be in a calm and peaceful condition. During this critical period, you should avoid seriously stressful conditions that may disrupt the healing process. Even after initial abstinence, your brain still needs time to stabilize, the healing process may span more than one or two years.

Brain Exercises (Main Session)

 1 Answer these questions.

a. What did you eat for breakfast this morning?
b. Where did you go last weekend and what did you do?
c. What was the name of the movie you have recently seen?

 2 Complete the following sayings.

a. When in _____ , do _____ the Romans
b. Hope for _____ , but _____ for the worst
c. Keep your friends _____ and your _____ closer
d. Never look a _____ horse in the _____
e. You can't make an _____ without _____ a few eggs

 3 Match a word on the first row with a word on the second row to form a complete word.

| wall | door | earth | ham | cup |
| burger | flower | board | bell | worm |

 4 Look at the below symbols for 10 seconds and then turn to the next page.(The order of symbols is important)

Without returning to the previous page, answer the below questions.
a. Which symbol comes after ⓡ ?
b. In which below option, the order of three symbols are the same as one in previous page?

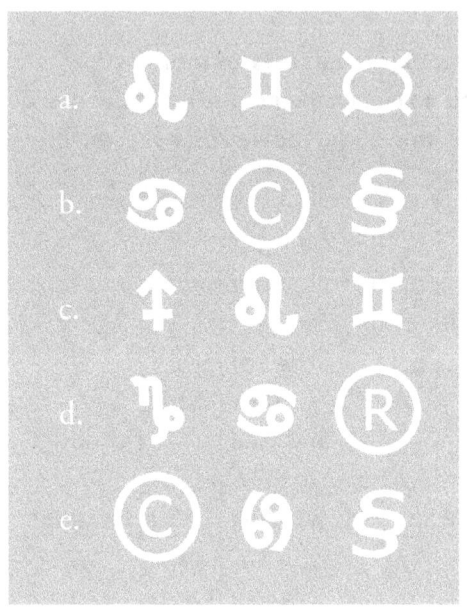

c. Which symbol comes between ♊ and ♌ ?

5 Look at the below list of words for 10 seconds and then turn to the next page.

clock	hand	book
tree	job	white
friend	fork	car

Without returning to the previous page, answer these questions.
a. Write the first two words of the first row.
b. Write the words in the second column.
c. Write the last two words of third column.

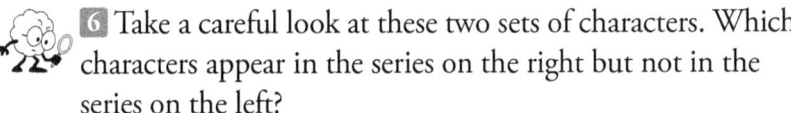
6 Take a careful look at these two sets of characters. Which characters appear in the series on the right but not in the series on the left?

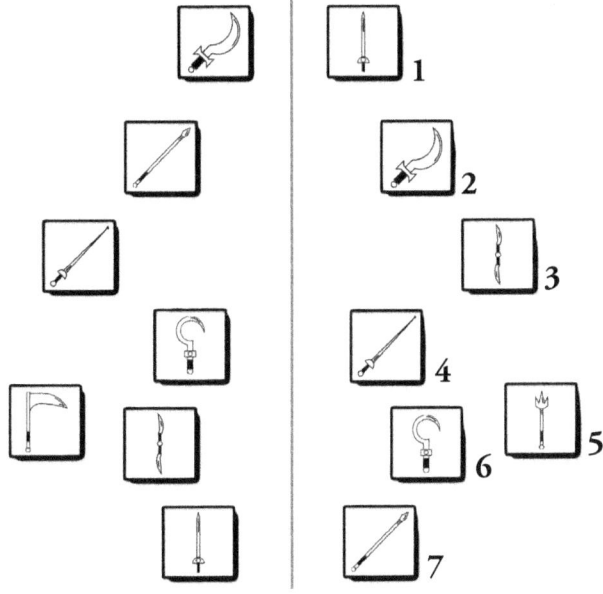

7 Look at the below pictures for 10 seconds and then turn to the next page.

Without returning to the previous page, try to recall as many pictures as you can.

8 Try to solve the below Sudoku puzzle and note that each row, column, and nonet (sections of nine bordered cells) can contain each number (typically 1 to 9) exactly once

4	8		7		2		9	5
9			4		8	2		7
7		2	9	5		4	6	
6		9		8	4		2	1
8		1	3			9		6
	5	7		9		8	4	
1	2		6			3		9
	9			7	1		8	
5		4	8	3		6		2

9 Look at the below pictures for 15 seconds and then turn to the next page.

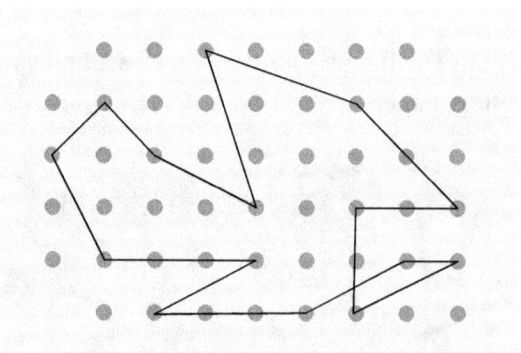

Without returning to the previous page, try to complete the picture by drawing lines.

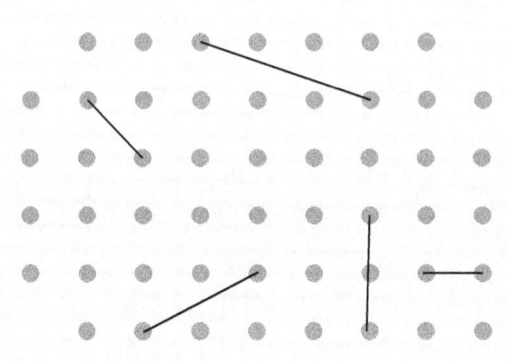

10 What picture should replace the question mark?

Part 1

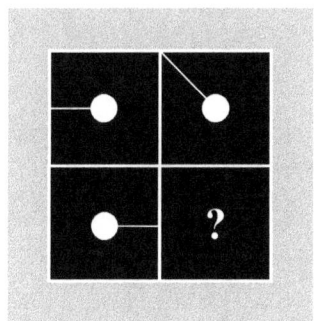

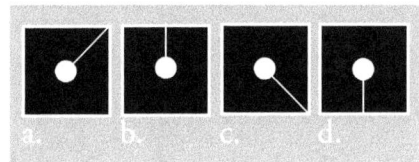

Part 2

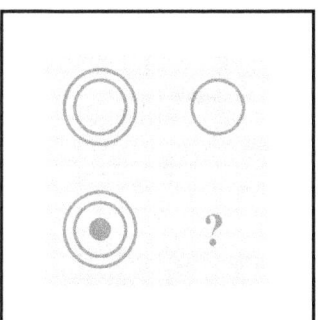

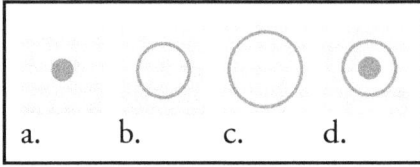

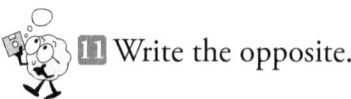 **11** Write the opposite.

a. Poor
b. Beautiful
c. Winner
d. Borrowing
e. Appear
f. Asleep

12 Determine the fewest number of moves necessary to change the configuration in Figure A to that shown in Figure B. You may not place a larger disk on a smaller one, and you may move only one disk at a time.

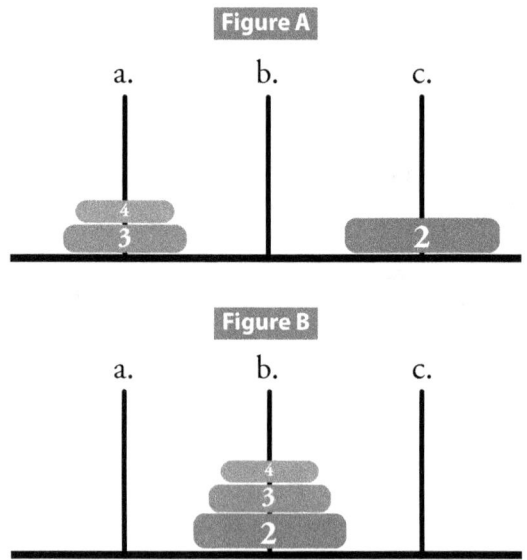

Number of movements:

Report Card

Date   Number of incorrect answers   Time duration
Main weak points

Conclusion

Extra Exercises (Home-work)

 1 Complete the following sayings.

a. Don't bite the ____ that feeds ____
b. Beauty is in the ____ of the beholder
c. ____ is the mother of invention
d. You can't ____ a book by its cover
e. Good things ____ to those who ____

 2 Find the right connection between brands and productions.

Sandwiches	○	○ Toyota
Home accessories	○	○ Toblerone
Camera	○	○ IKEA
Car	○	○ Subway
Chocolate	○	○ Canon

 3 Look at the below pictures for 10 seconds and then turn to the next page.

1.   2.   3.   4.   5.   6.   7.   8.   9.

Without returning to the previous page, answer these questions.

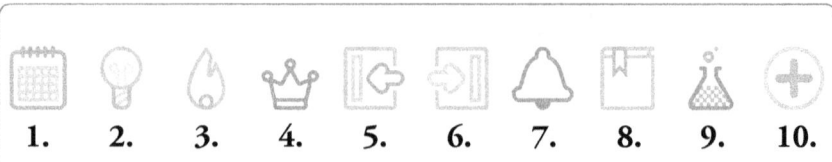

a. Compared to the picture in the previous page, which icon has been appeared in the above picture.

b. Which two icons have been changed in color?

c. Which two icons have been changed their place?

4 Look at the below pictures for 15 seconds and then turn to the next page.

a. **Without returning to the previous page, try to recall all of the water sports.**

b. **Which sport is located above basketball?**

c. **Write the name of the team sport pictured.**

5 Match two words to form a complete word. Noted that each word should be used just once.

brush	copy	high	six	break
new	time	gold	out	sand
Fast	ice	hair	wich	photo
standing	teen	cream	light	born

6 Look at the below pictures for 15 seconds and then turn to the next page.

Without returning to the previous page, try to recall as many pictures as you can.

7 Try to write as many word as you can in 60 seconds, using the last letter of former word as the first letter of the latter word. see the example.
Cat, Tea, Apple,

8 Try to solve the below Sudoku puzzle and note that each row, column, and nonet (sections of nine bordered cells) can contain each number (typically 1 to 9) exactly once

	7			5		8		9
4		5	7		9		3	
1	9			4				7
	4	2	8		6		5	3
3			9			6		
5	6	9		2	3		7	8
		1		8		7	9	
	2		6		7	3		
9		7	1			4		6

9 What picture should replace the question marks?

Part 1

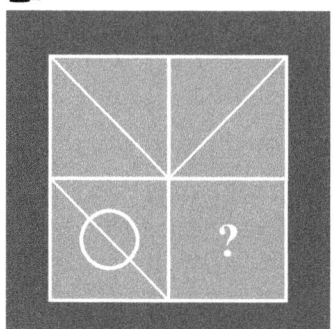
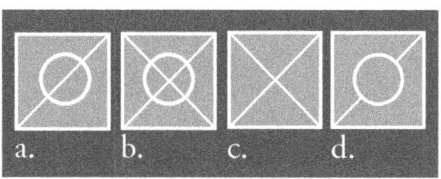

Part 2

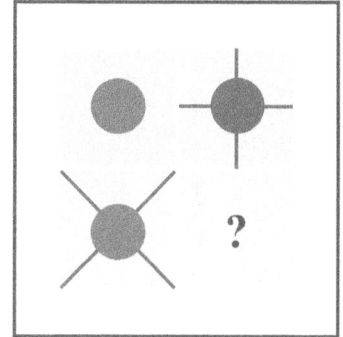
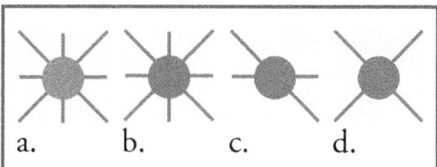

 10 Write the opposite.

a. **Lazy**
b. **Healthy**
c. **Expensive**
d. **Clean**
e. **Rainy**
f. **Kindness**

11. Determine the fewest number of moves necessary to change the configuration in Figure A to that shown in Figure B. You may not place a larger disk on a smaller one, and you may move only one disk at a time.

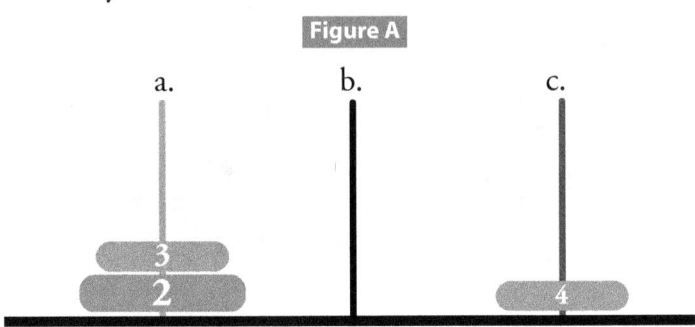

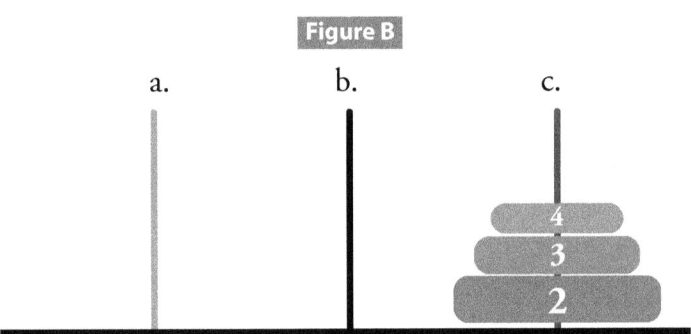

Number of movements:

12 Join the complementary figures.

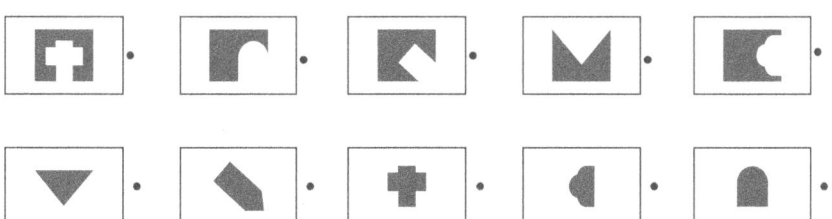

 13 To reach the point where the triangle is located, how many right and left turns must you make from the circle.

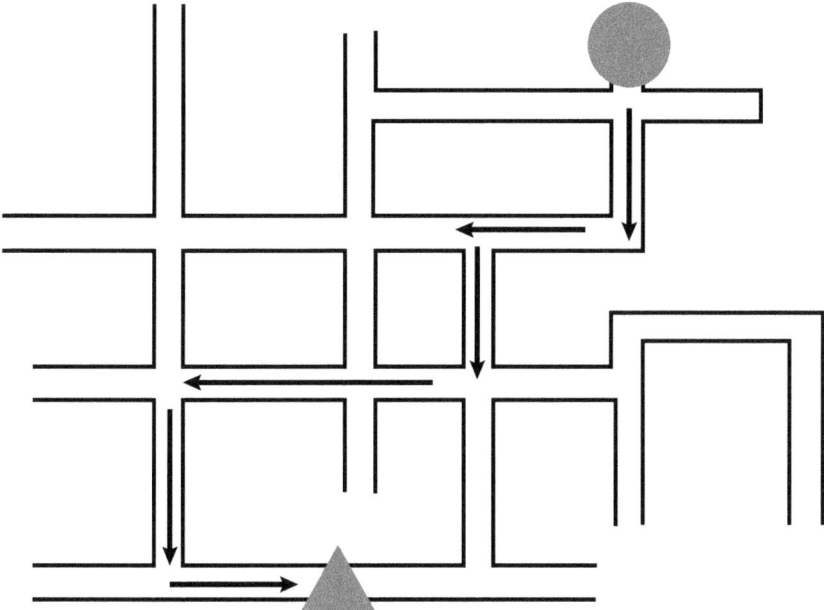

Number of turns to the left: ....
Number of turns to the right: ....

14 Try to find the names of determined animals in the below crossword table.

R	F	S	R	I	H	C	H	I	C	K	E	N	O
K	K	H	C	H	A	Y	G	T	O	N	P	K	B
H	T	E	O	M	A	K	A	G	O	O	S	E	B
A	U	E	P	E	C	E	A	L	O	L	H	B	B
H	R	P	I	K	T	A	O	G	B	H	N	I	F
O	K	N	G	A	A	N	G	G	P	F	S	H	G
A	E	A	E	B	A	S	E	E	R	O	E	P	I
H	Y	L	B	S	U	O	O	C	N	G	L	C	P
O	E	F	B	C	M	F	O	E	O	O	T	S	E
R	H	D	U	C	K	S	F	R	Y	S	T	W	M
S	M	L	L	A	M	A	C	A	F	P	A	O	H
E	L	A	M	B	E	P	S	S	L	E	C	C	G
E	O	P	N	U	C	L	U	T	Y	O	U	N	M
B	U	S	O	B	H	L	L	T	B	T	A	G	C

BUFFALO
GOAT
BISON
PIG
DUCK
GOOSE
CATTLE
SHEEP
CHICKEN
HORSE
TURKEY
LAMB
COW
LLAMA

Report Card

Date   Number of incorrect answers   Time duration

Main weak points

Conclusion

Brain Club
7th Session

 **Brain Education**

1 Who can help me in the Process of Brain Recovery?

During the process of brain recovery, you need a therapist or counselor as a coach who helps train your brain gradually and helps you to apply some useful techniques and strategies to cope with brain dysfunctions. Your coach, as an expert brain trainer, prescribes you a proper set of exercises and teaches you how you can change your lifestyle to support your brain health.

2 Is there any medicine I can use for speeding up Brain Recovery?

There is no specific medication available, yet, to fully reconstruct brain recovery. There might be some medications that can be helpful for brain recovery, but only under guidance and direction from your addiction-knowledgeable physician or psychiatrist. Any medicine used during your recovery should be doctor-prescribed and used very carefully as to not create more struggles for your "in-recovery" brain.

Brain Exercises (Main Session)

 １ Try to find all hidden items in the picture and circle them.

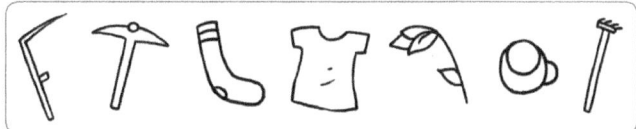

2 Try to find all hidden items in the picture and circle them.

3 In this exercise, you can see different boxes including numbers with different repetitions. For the first part of exercise, read just the number but for the second part accurately identify the number of repetitions for each number. Record your time for both parts and compare them.

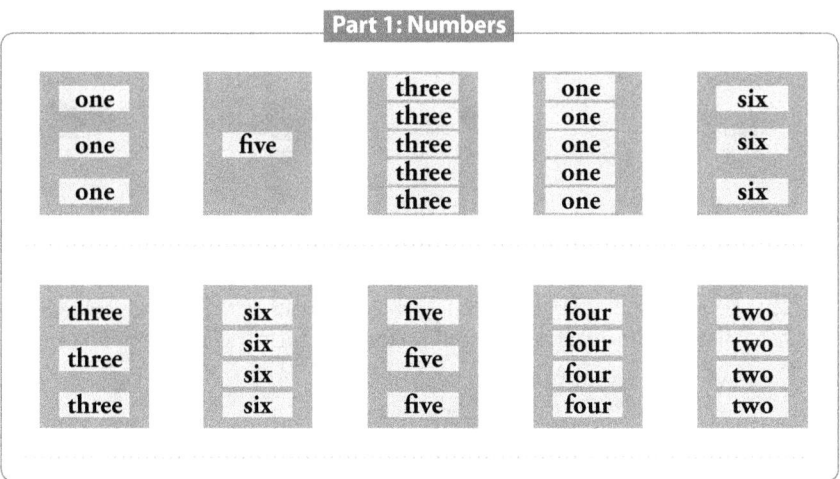

Time (sec): ....   Number of errors: ....

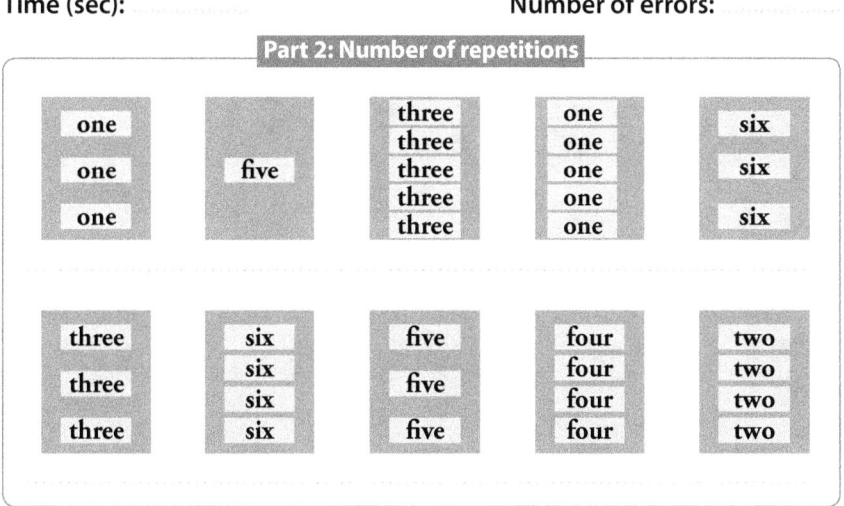

Time (sec): ....   Number of errors: ....

4 Look at the faces below and try to identify the emotion conveyed in each face.

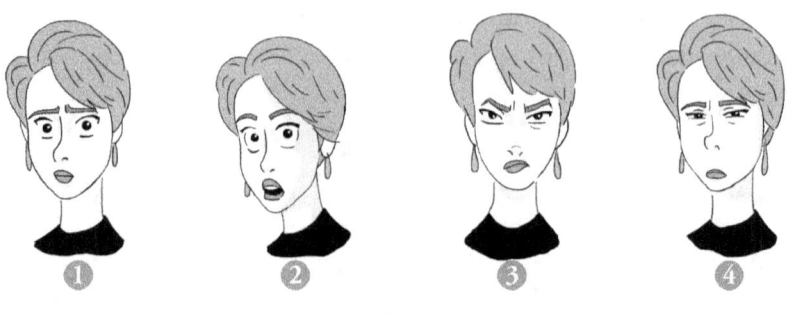

5 Scan the below images and try to find as many as target pictures and mark them as indentified for each target picture. Write the total number.

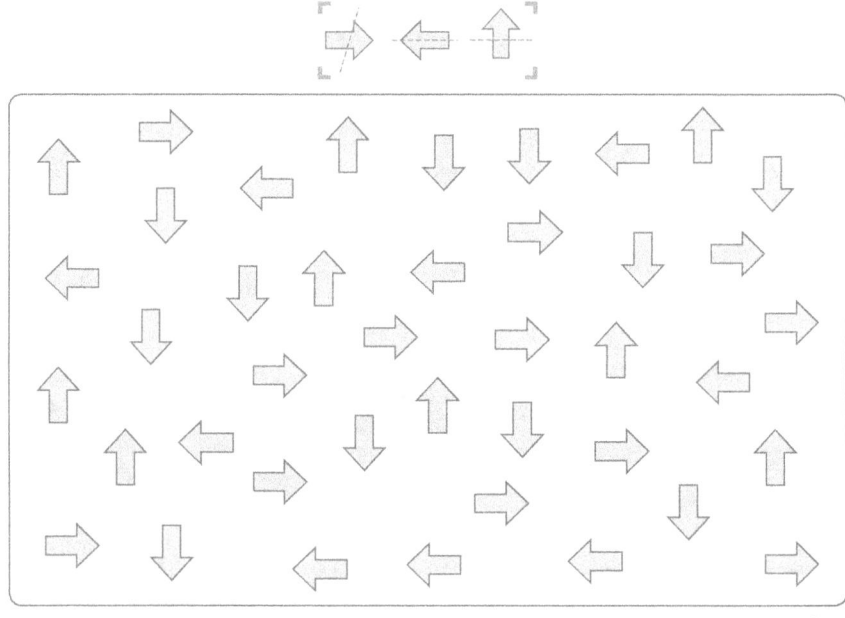

Total number: .... ➡   Total number: .... ⬅   Total number: .... ⬆

6 Look carefully at the following two pairs of images and try to spot differences.

7 differences

7 Look carefully at the following two pairs of images and try to spot differences.

11 differences

 8 Calculate equations below and write the answers.

a. 3 + 9 + 7 =

b. 120 ÷ 4 ÷ 6 =

c. 329 + 457 =

d. 2 × 5 × 43 =

e. 20 × 30 - 30 =

f. 20 × 25 + 60 =

g. 101 × 7 =

h. 243 + 6 =

i. 1000 ÷ 25 =

j. 741 - 164 =

k. 321 × 2 =

l. 6/6 ÷ 2/2 =

m. 666 + 111 =

n. 91 + 205 =

 **9** Complete the table with proper numbers.

					2				2		
				8	÷		=	4	+		
		3	7		1						
			+			=	4	×		=	4
		9	×	8	=			×		8	
		=						0			
		1		1	+		−	6	=		9
5		2		2		+			0	5	÷
×				=		3			÷		3
	−		=	3		=		4	5	÷	= 5
=									=		×
4		÷					+	3	=	6	7
0		7									=
		=									
							1	2	−		=

 10 What number should replace the question mark?

3	1	4
2	5	1
3	2	?

Date   Number of incorrect answers   Time duration
Main weak points

Conclusion

Extra Exercises (Home-work)

1 Try to find all hidden items in the picture and circle them.

2 Try to find all hidden items in the picture and circle them.

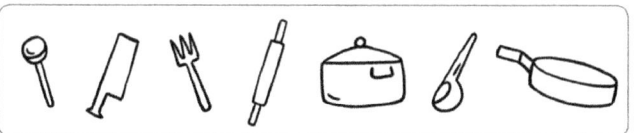

3 In this exercise, you can see different boxes including numbers with different repetitions. For the first part of exercise, read just the number but for the second part accurately identify the number of repetitions for each number. Record your time for both parts and compare them.

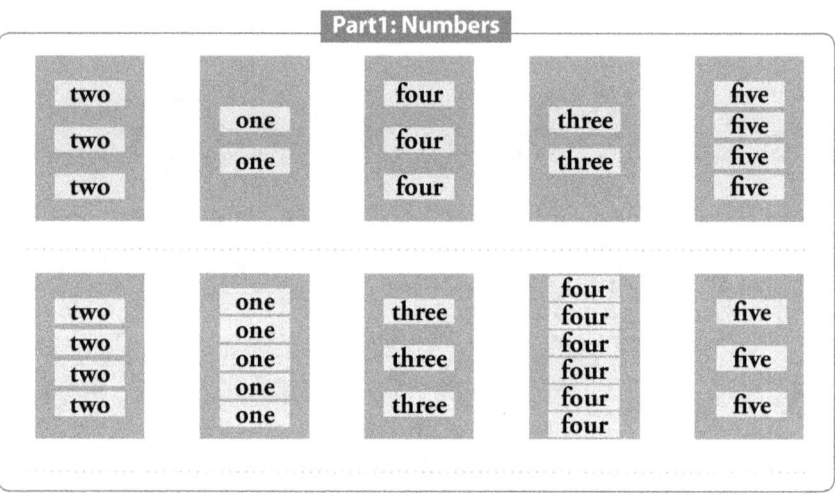

Time (sec): _____   Number of errors: _____

Time (sec): _____   Number of errors: _____

4 Look at the faces below and try to identify the emotion conveyed in each face.

   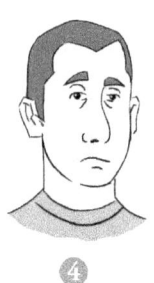

① ② ③ ④

 5 Scan the below images and try to find as many as target pictures and mark the total of target pictures. Write the total number.

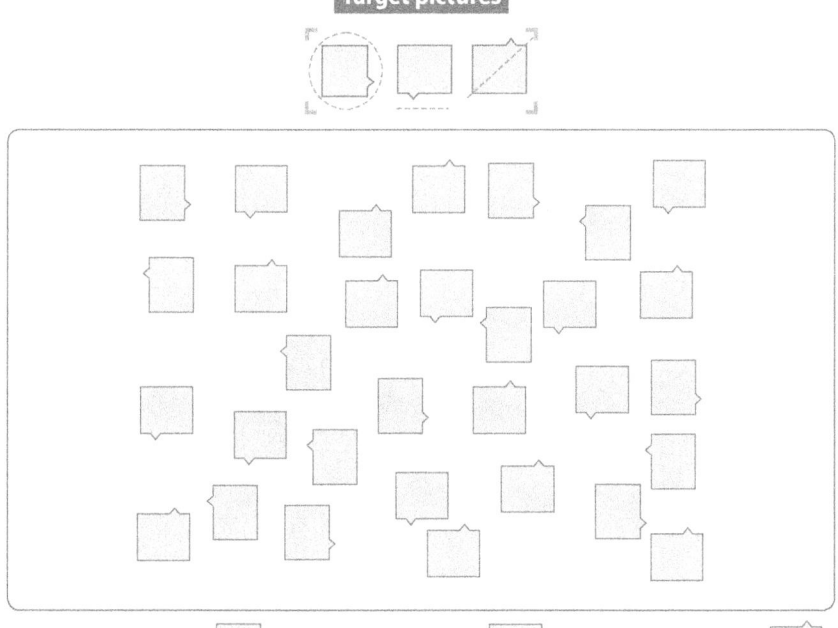

Total number: _____   Total number: _____   Total number: _____

6 Determine the minimum number of moves needed to move from the configuration in Figure A to the configuration in Figure B. Follow these rules:
- Balls may move out of baskets only upward.
- You may not place more than three balls in one basket.
- You may move only one ball at a time

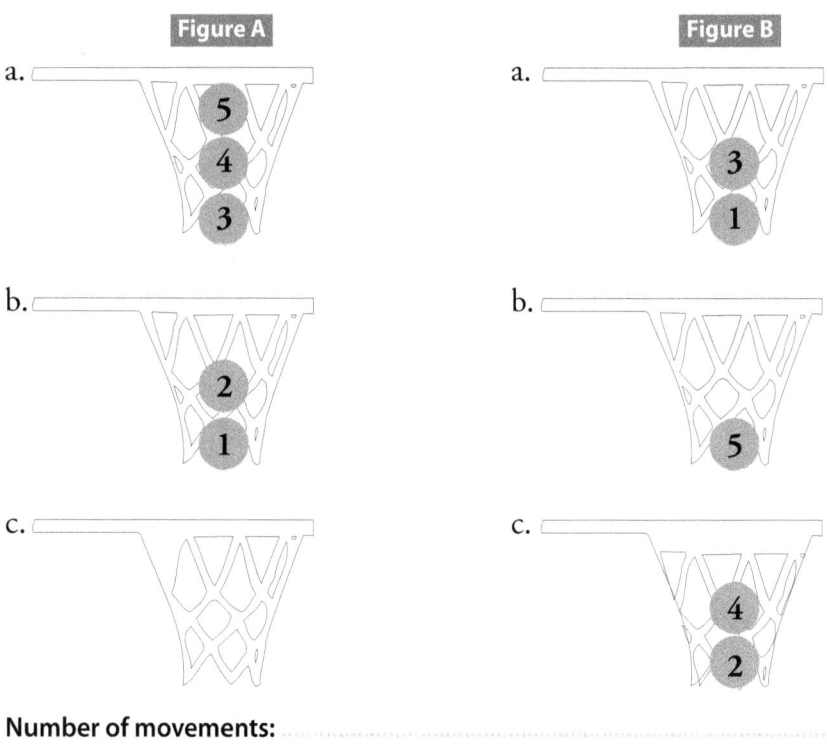

Number of movements: ....

7 Look carefully at the following two pairs of images and try to spot differences.

15 differences

 8 What numbers should replace the question marks?

4	7	3
5	?	4
9	?	7

a. 9, 15
b. 8, 19
c. 9, 16
d. 8, 15

9 What numbers should replace the question mark?

a.

6	2	7		5	3	7
5	2	6		7	2	8
8	1	8		6	8	?

b.

	5			13			8	
6	4	7	8	4	17	11	7	?

10 What number should replace the question mark to continue the sequence?

a. 1, 11, 20, 28, 35, 41, ?

b. 5, 10, 11, 22, 23, ?

c. 100, 91, 73, 64, 46, 37, ?

d. 7, 15, 31, 63, 127, ?

e. 3, 6, 11, ?, ?, 54, 59, 118,

f. 524, 526, 528, 530, ?

Report Card

Date   **Number of incorrect answers**   **Time duration**

Main weak points

Conclusion

Brain Club
8th Session

Brain Education

1 Are there any therapeutic services that directly target my Brain Injuries?

Cognitive rehabilitation is a newly entered therapeutic intervention in the field of addiction medicine. Cognitive rehabilitation directly targets brain functions such as attention, memory and decision making which are impaired due to drug abuse. Cognitive rehabilitation consists of a series of exercises and strategies which are applied to restore brain power over time. Cognitive rehabilitation is a customized treatment which can be administered either in group or individual setting. Recent studies show that cognitive rehabilitation might even help you to maintain sobriety.

2 How can I know that I am getting better?

Brain functions are needed for every task we do in our everyday life including driving, studying, writing, cooking, speaking to our friends and so much more. Once our brain isn't working properly, we may face problems even in very simple tasks. So, after you start the cognitive rehabilitation process, you should see the changes occur gradually in your everyday life. Your family members may also notice these changes.

Brain Exercises (Main Session)

 1 Read the below paragraphs and find the letters specified for each part. Note that you should find letters simultaneously.

A. Letters "G/g" and "N/n"

Eggplant is an unusual vegetable that has a unique range of health benefits, including an ability to help build strong bones and prevent osteoporosis, reduce symptoms of anemia, increase cognitive function, improve cardiovascular health, protect the digestive system, help lose weight, manage diabetes, reduce stress, protect infants from birth defects, and even prevent cancer. There are a number of varieties used throughout the world, and they are included in cuisines in many different ways. It is commonly called the "king of vegetables", at least in India, as it is one of the most versatile and functional foods in the cultural gamut. It has the consistency of tomato, in terms of texture and density, and it is a perfect addition to soups, stews, sauces, as well as a stand-alone item in many dishes. The best part about the food, it is not only a flavorful and delicious addition to many meals, but also a massively healthy vegetable that can help you live a healthier and happier life.

Number of letters "G/g" and "N/n":

B. Letters "M/m" and "P/p"

The heart is a muscular organ in humans and other animals, which pumps blood through the blood vessels of the circulatory system. Blood provides the body with oxygen and nutrients, as well as assists in the removal of metabolic wastes. In humans, the heart is located between the lungs, in the middle compartment of the chest. In humans, other mammals, and birds, the heart is divided into four chambers: upper left and right atria; and lower left and right ventricles. Commonly the right atrium and ventricle are referred together as the right heart and their left counterparts as the left heart. Fish, in contrast, have two chambers, an atrium and a ventricle, while reptiles have three chambers. In a healthy heart blood flows one way through the heart due to heart valves, which prevent backflow. The heart is enclosed in a protective sac, the pericardium, which also contains a small amount of fluid. The wall of the heart is made up of three layers: epicardium, myocardium, and endocardium. The heart pumps blood with a rhythm determined by a group of pacemaking cells in the sinoatrial node. These generate a current that causes contraction of the heart, traveling through the atrioventricular node and along the conduction system of the heart.

Number of letters "M/m" and "P/p":

2 Link the circles and triangles consecutively, without raising your pencil. Note that you can not touch squares and you can not pass through each circle and triangle more than once.

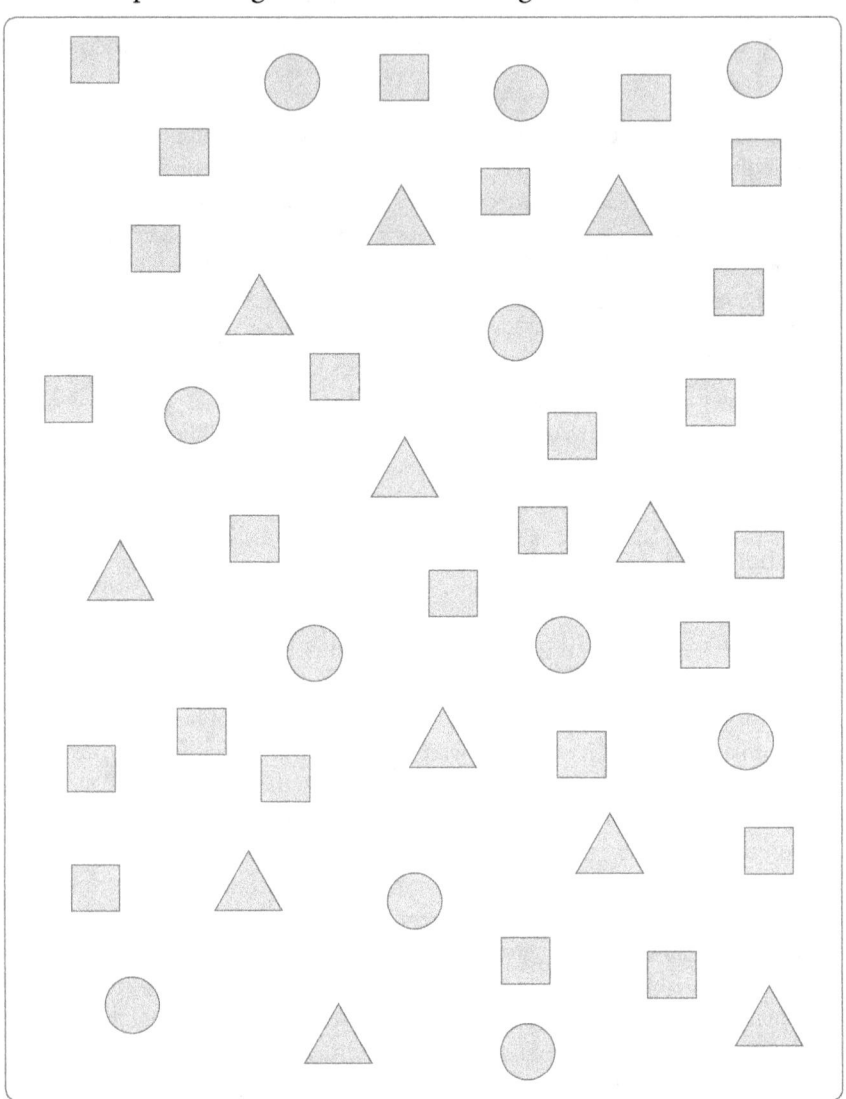

Time (sec):

3 Try to find a path between the gray and pink arrows that joins the entrance and the exit parts of the path.

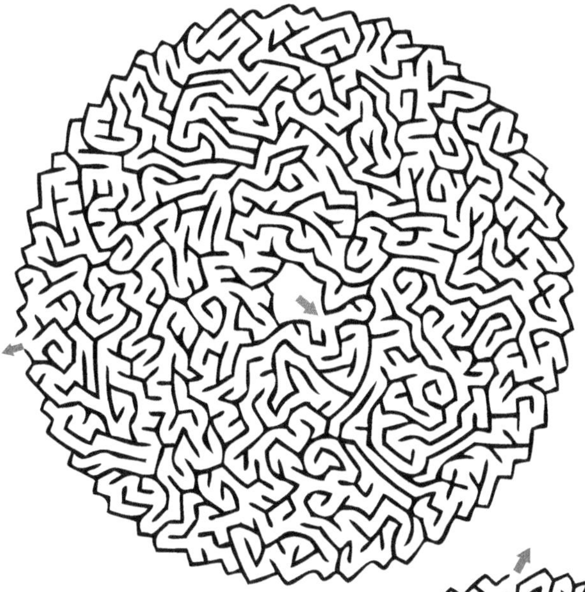

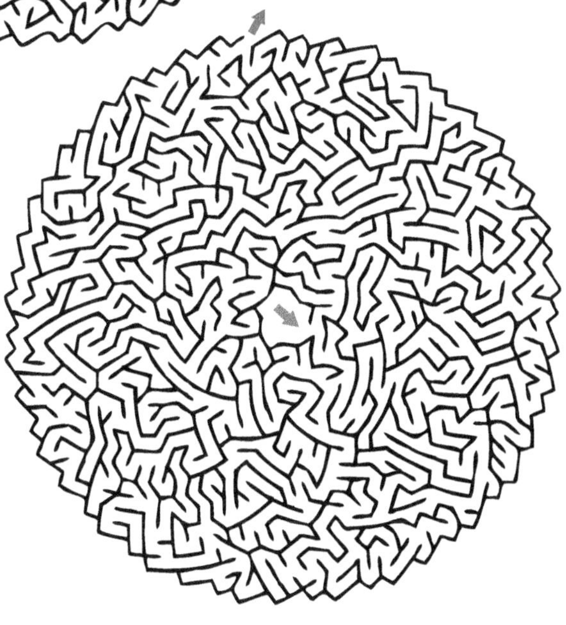

4 Find the odd one in this series.

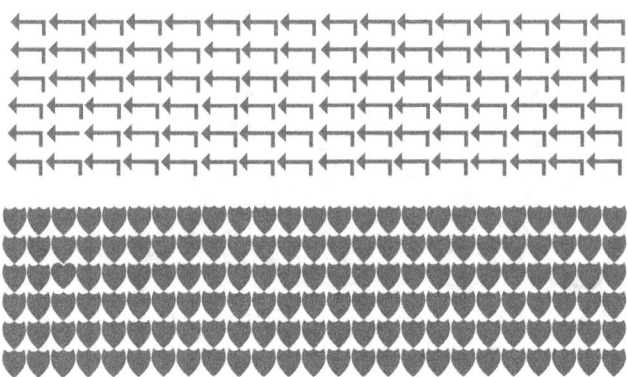

 5 See the figure below; then determine which three of the nine figures below are combined to form the main figure.

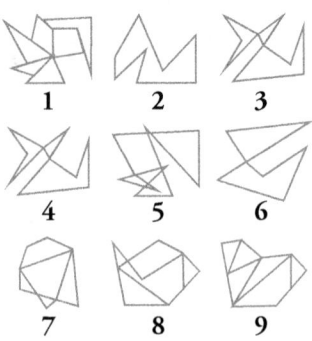

6 To reach the point where the triangle is located, how many right and left turns must you make from the circle.

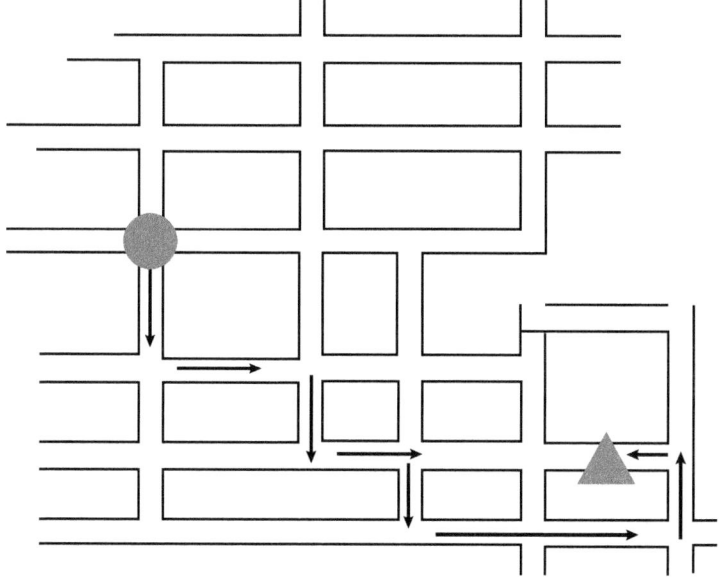

Number of turns to the left:
Number of turns to the right:

 7 How many triangles are in this picture?

Number of triangles:

8 Look at the below picture and try to find all number "2" that follow after ✚. Record the total number.

1	❖	3	2	✚	1	1	❖	2	✚	1	2	4	✚	3
❖	2	❖	2	✚	2	4	✚	1	2	✚	1	1	✚	2
✚	2	❖	1	3	✚	3	3	✚	2	❖	3	✚	3	❖
❖	5	✚	2	4	❖	1	❖	2	4	❖	2	3	2	✚
2	✚	2	1	❖	3	❖	2	❖	4	4	2	✚	2	3
1	✚	3	✚	4	✚	2	1	❖	2	✚	4	2	2	✚
✚	5	3	❖	✚	5	2	❖	✚	2	3	1	✚	2	1
3	2	✚	2	1	❖	2	✚	4	3	❖	2	1	2	✚
5	✚	2	1	❖	4	5	✚	3	2	✚	1	❖	2	1
✚	3	❖	5	2	5	✚	2	❖	3	2	✚	5	❖	1
2	3	✚	2	2	❖	5	✚	2	3	✚	2	4	✚	❖

Number of "2": _____

Date   **Number of incorrect answers**   **Time duration**

Main weak points

Conclusion

Report Card

Extra Exercises (Home-work)

 1 Read the below paragraphs and find the letters specified for each part. Note that you should find letters simultaneously.

Letters "B/b" and "W/w"

Rabbits are small mammals in the family Leporidae of the order Lagomorpha, found in several parts of the world. There are eight different genera in the family classified as rabbits, including the European rabbit , cottontail rabbits , and the Amami rabbit . There are many other species of rabbit, and these, along with pikas and hares, make up the order Lagomorpha. Rabbit habitats include meadows, woods, forests, grasslands, deserts and wetlands. Rabbits live in groups, and the best known species, the European rabbit, lives in underground burrows, or rabbit holes. A group of burrows is called a warren. More than half the world›s rabbit population resides in North America.They are also native to southwestern Europe, Southeast Asia, Sumatra, some islands of Japan, and in parts of Africa and South America. They are not naturally found in most of Eurasia, where a number of species of hares are present. Rabbits first entered South America relatively recently, as part of the Great American Interchange. Much of the continent has just one species of rabbit, the tapeti, while most of South America›s southern cone is without rabbits. The rabbit›s long ears, which can be more than 10 cm long, are probably an adaptation for detecting predators. They have large, powerful hind legs. The two front paws have 5 toes, the extra called the dewclaw. The hind feet have 4 toes. They are plantigrade animals while at rest; however, they move around on their toes while running, assuming a more digitigrade form. Unlike some other paw structures of quadruped mammals, especially those of domesticated pets, rabbit paws lack pads. Their nails are strong and are used for digging; along with their teeth, they are also used for defense

Number of letters "B/b" and "W/w":

2 Read the below paragraphs and find the letters specified for each part. Note that you should find letters simultaneously

Letters "R/r" and "U/u"

Among all the health benefits of calcium, the most important ones are that it aids in maintaining bone health and dental health, as well as the prevention of colon cancer and the reduction of obesity. We need it from birth all the way until we reach old age. In our infant days, it is required for proper bone and tooth growth; during adolescence, as the bones develop, calcium is again essential to support the growth. Finally, when we get older, our bones tend to get porous and weak, thereby requiring ample calcium intake. With so many fancy diets around us, we often tend to avoid calcium-rich foods like whole food groups, including dairy products. This avoidance often results in its deficiency. Reports say that calcium deficiency conditions are continuously rising, particularly in women who are on low-calorie diets to get slim, and are therefore confronted with the threat or trouble of osteoporosis. Thus, it is extremely important to consume enough calcium, vitamin D, magnesium, and K2 throughout your tender and adolescence years. Calcium forms 2% of total body weight in a human adult. It is found in the human body as deposits in the bones and teeth in high volumes. Traces of the mineral are also present in the circulatory system, which prevent life threatening hemorrhages. calcium is easily available in milk and dairy products like cheese and yogurt. Furthermore, nuts, tinned salmon, seeds and pulses are good sources of calcium.

Number of letters "R/r" and "U/u": ....

3 Link the circles with even numbers and triangles consecutively, without raising your pencil. Note that you can not touch any other circles and you can not pass through each desired circle and triangle more than once.

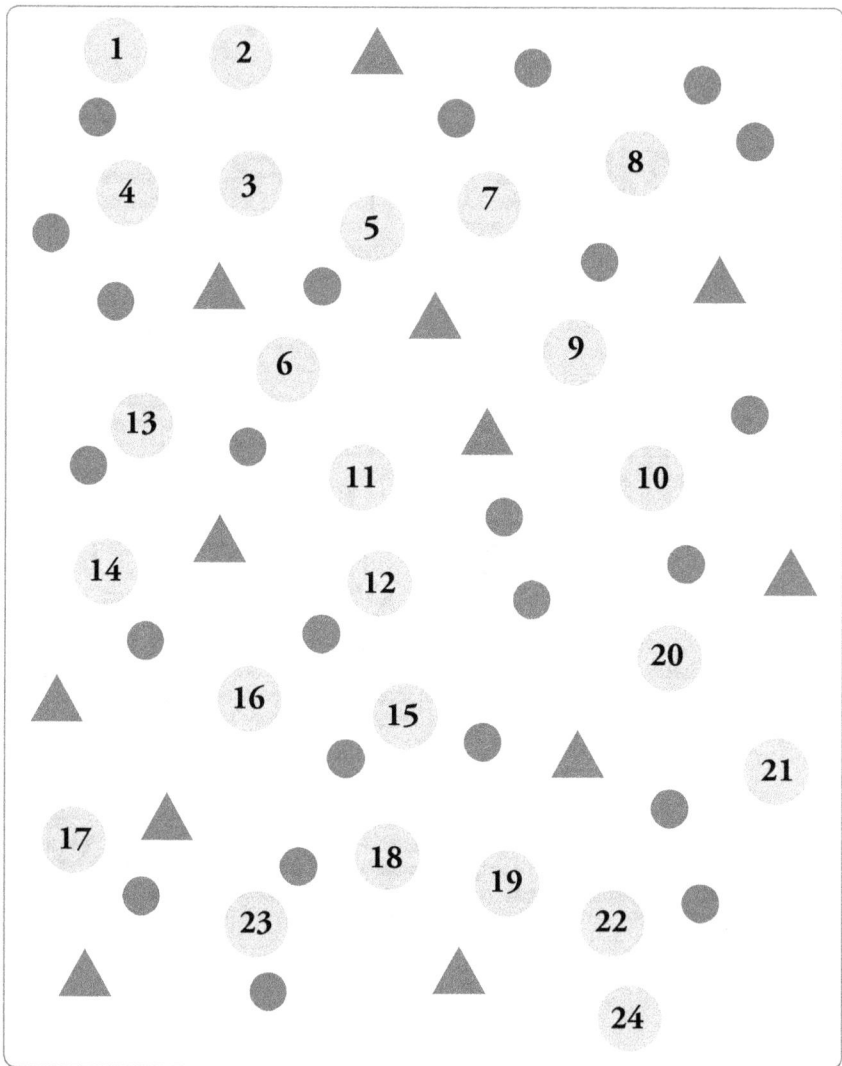

Time (sec):

4 Try to find a path between the gray and pink arrows that joins the entrance and the exit parts of the path.

5 Which of the four tiles doesn't belong to the picture?

  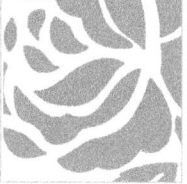 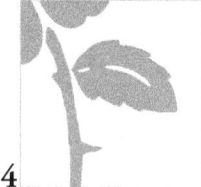
1 2 3 4

 6 Find the odd one in this series.

RRRRRRRRRRRRRRRRRRRRRRRRRRRR
RRRRRRRRRRRRRRRRRRRRRRRRRRRR
RRRRRRRRRRRRRRRRRRRRRRRRRRRR
RRRRRRRRRRRRRRRRRRRRRRRRRRRR
RRRRRPRRRRRRRRRRRRRRRRRRRRRR
RRRRRRRRRRRRRRRRRRRRRRRRRRRR

7 See the figure below; then determine which three of the nine figures below are combined to form the main figure.

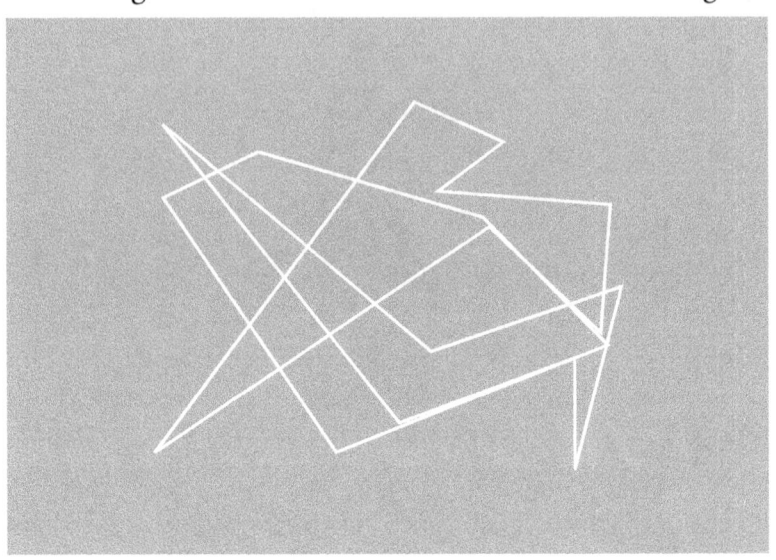

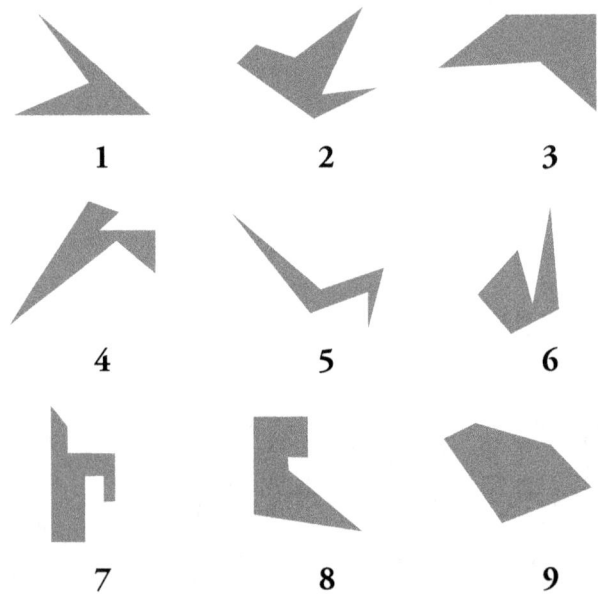

1   2   3

4   5   6

7   8   9

8 Look at the below picture. One tile is missing. Select the missing piece.

a.

b.

c.

9 How many squares are in this picture?

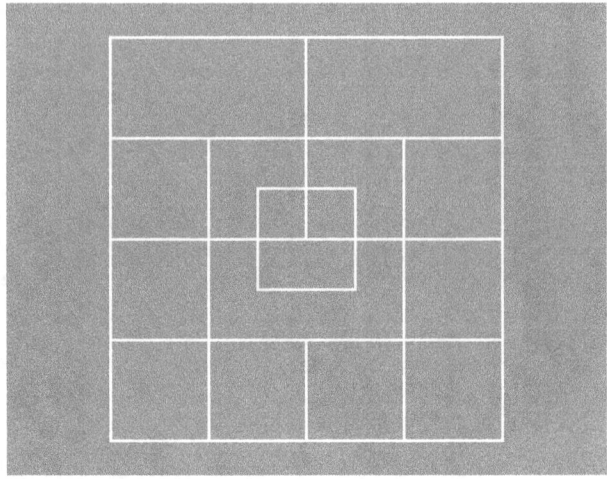

 10 Draw the other half of the picture.

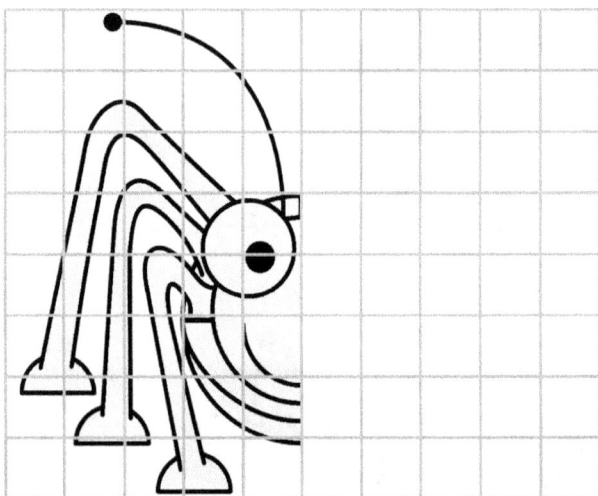

Date   **Number of incorrect answers**   **Time duration**

Main weak points

Conclusion

Brain Club
9th Session

 **Brain Education**

1 Does my brain recovery take place automatically during abstinence?

During the phase of abstinence, as your brain does not receive any toxic substances, your brain automatically starts to show improvements in some aspects of functions. But for a comprehensive recovery, abstinence might not be sufficient for all former drug users; therefore, you might need to participate in cognitive rehabilitation exercises to expose your brain with systematic and structured experiences. These tasks are designed to specifically activate different regions of your brain and increase their performances.

2 Is there anything that I can do to facilitate my brain recovery other than brain exercises?

Besides doing a brain training program, provided by your therapist or counsellor, there are other issues that if appropriately addressed and applied in the context of real life, they could facilitate your brain recovery. For example, your daily diet, sleeping time, physical activity and social interaction have important roles in the speed of brain recovery.

Brain Exercises (Main Session)

1 Write one synonym for each word.

a. Final   b. Tradition

c. Teacher   d. Imagination

e. Smile   f. Jungle

2 Write one antonym for each word.

a. Finding   b. Destroyed

c. Dark   d. Strange

e. Miserable   f. Often

3 Look at the directions below for 10 seconds and then turn to the next page.

Start from number 2, Go to number 7, Turn right, Now, go downward, Then, turn left, Go upward, Go number 3, Turn left one more time, Return to number 7

Without returning to previous page, mark the picture which is indicated in the directions you have read in previous page.

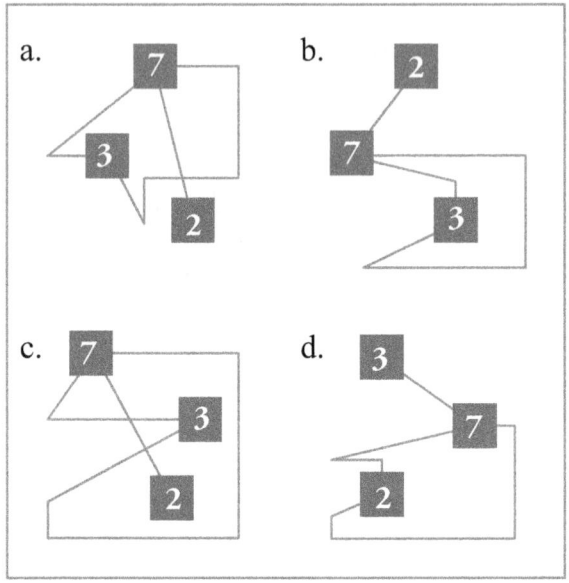

4 Take a careful look at these two sets of characters. Which characters appear in the series on the right but not in the series on the left?

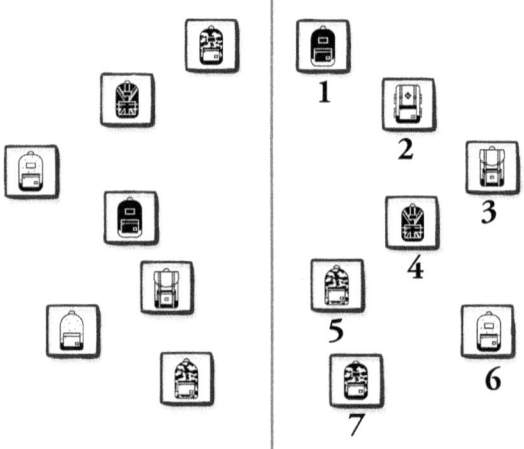

 **5** Try to complete the crossword.

Across

1. Worn on the head- 4. Italian wine city- 8. "Get outta here!" 12. Half: Prefix- 13. Avenue or boulevard- 14. Bank caper 16. Spoken- 17. Calm- 18. City on the Rhone- 19. Wt. units 20. Talent for music- 21. Calendar pg- 23. Vane dir- 24. Written report- 26. Make do- 28. Bumped into- 30. "___ching"- 32. Table supports- 36. Edible seaweed- 39. Proficient- 41. Flames 42. Seventh Greek letter- 43. Saloon fight- 45. Actress ___ Dawn Chong- 46. Apiece- 48. Tolstoy's Karenina- 49. Department store sign- 50. An entreaty- 51. Writing liquid- 52. Graphy or logy prefix- 54. Doctor (slang)- 56. Likeness- 60. Long period of time 63. Commandments number- 65. Texting abbr for oversharing 67. Morsel- 68. Depleted- 70. Niagra river source- 72. Spoiled kid 73. Fixed gaze- 74. Departed- 75. Italian mount- 76. Our sun is one- 77. Eyelid infection- 78. Father

Down

1. Rosemary and thyme- 2. Accumulate- 3. "Shop ___ you drop" 4. Specialty- 5. Fly high- 6. Profs aides- 7. New thought- 8. Ocean predator- 9. That lady- 10. Lubricates- 11. Sugar suffixes- 12. Food fish- 15. Philsopher lao ___ - 20. See with it- 22. Small round veggie- 25. Hi-fi component- 27. Santa's helper- 29. Computer key near capslock- 30. Sword-on-armor sound- 31. Chopped down 33. Emerald isle- 34. Mom's mom for short- 35. Notices- 36. Hold on to- 37. list ending abbr- 38. Frilly fabric- 40. Cereal grain 44. Chem room- 47. Owned- 49. May honoree- 51. Frozen water 53. Clock numeral- 55. Web-footed mammal- 57. Main heart artery- 58. Kind of piano- 59- Blues singer James- 60. Double curved letter- 61. Makes a choice- 62. Tidy- 64. Recent information 65. Very small- 66. Dole out- 69. Gun lobby grp- 71. Not in workforce anymore (abbr)- 72. Garden spot

6 Look at the below pictures for 20 seconds and then turn to the next page.

Without returning to the previous page, try to recall as many pictures as you can.

 7 Try to solve the below Sudoku puzzle and note that each row, column, and nonet (sections of nine bordered cells) can contain each number (typically 1 to 9) exactly once

1	3			7		5		
9		6		2			1	7
	7		9		4	3		
4	2		1	5		7		6
8		3		9		5		4
5		7		8	2		9	3
		1	8				4	
7	5		2			6		1
3		2		6	1			9

8 Determine the fewest number of moves necessary to change the configuration in Figure A to that shown in Figure B. You may not place a larger disk on a smaller one, and you may move only one disk at a time.

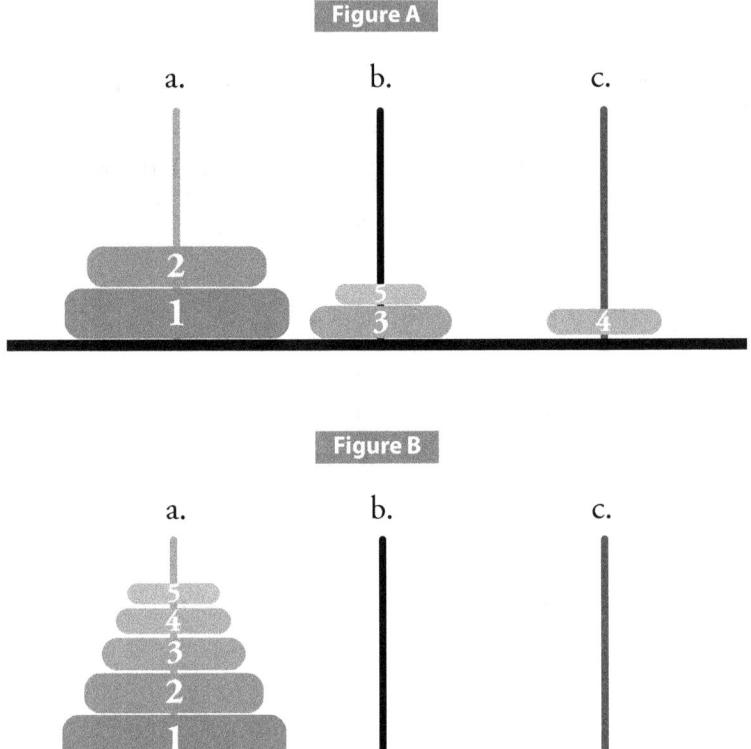

Number of movements:

 **9** Which picture should replace the question marks?

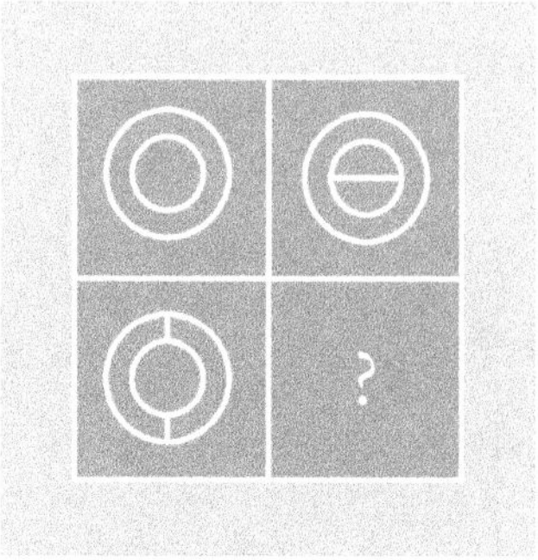

Part 1

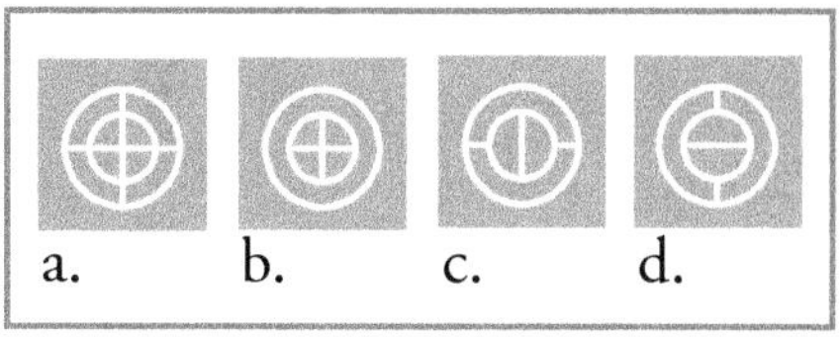

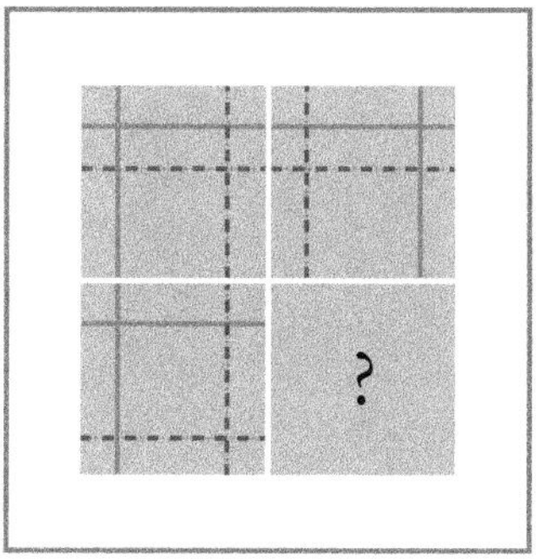

a. b. c. d.

Part 2

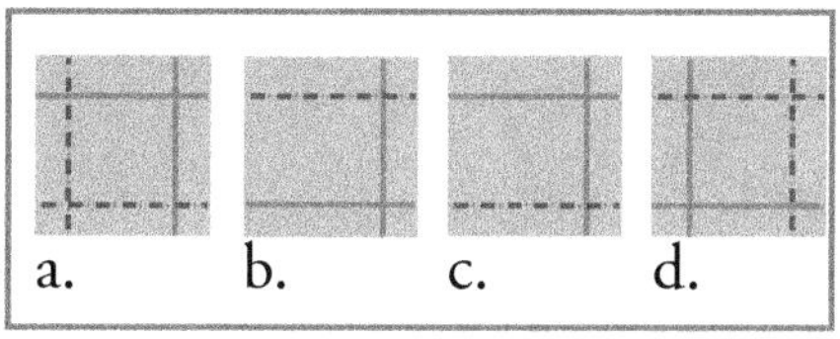

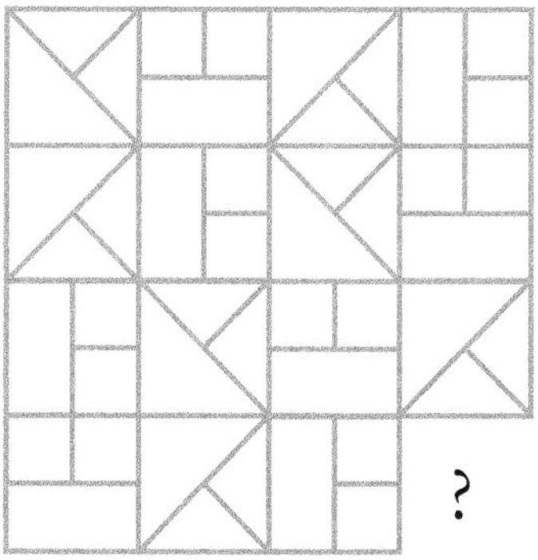

a. b. c. d.

Part 3

a. b. c. d. e.

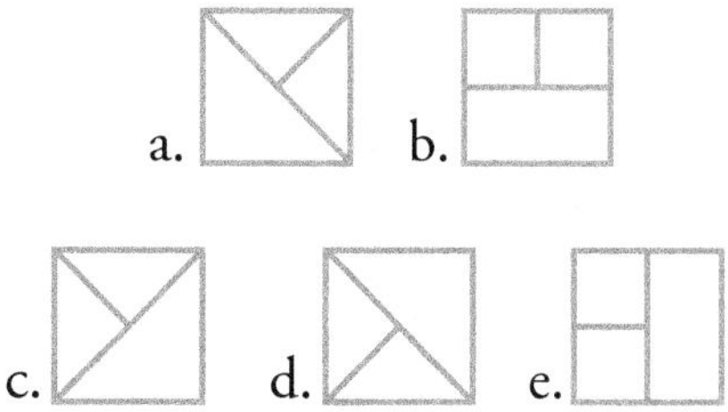

Date   Number of incorrect answers   Time duration
Main weak points

Conclusion

Report Card

Extra Exercises (Home-work)

 1 Write one synonym for each word.

a. Old .... b. Wise ....

c. Land .... d. Routine ....

e. Reward .... f. Wish ....

 2 Write one antonym for each word.

a. Peace .... b. Sad ....

c. Deprived .... d. Fact ....

e. Fast .... f. Dynamic ....

 3 Look at the below picture for 20 seconds and then turn to the next page.

146 | Brain Club

Without returning to the previous page answer these questions:

A. How many dresses was hang on hanger?
a. 4
b. 3
c. 2

B. What was not on the floor?
a. Yarn spool
b. Scissor
c. Box

C. What was on the table?
a. Glass
b. Flower
c. Cake

D. What was the girl doing?
a. Cutting fabric
b. Drinking tea
c. Tailoring clothes

 4 Try to complete the crossword.

Across

1. Sound of contempt- 4. Do this to fly- 8. Against- 12. 12:30 pm or 9:00 am- 13. Prefix with dynamic- 14. Eccentric- 16. Persia today 17. Water drops- 18. Worry- 19. Celtic sea god- 20. Break a commandment- 21. African antelope- 23. QB stats- 24. First name in cosmetics- 26. CPR expert- 28. Use it to catch butterflies -30. Tool with sharp teeth- 32. Broad ___ of a barn- 36. The beatles or The Who- 39. Not closed- 41. List ending abbr- 42. Make angry- 43. Needle tip- 45. Digital recordings- 46. Passed away- 48. Russian ruler- 49. Biblical you 50. Small whirlpool- 51. Put to work- 52. "___ go girl!"- 54. Blunder

56. Cloudburst- 60. Stern's opposite- 63. Small bill- 65. Compass dir 67. So-so grade- 68. Kind of potato- 70. Hallo ___ - 72. It holds up the flower- 73. They make you yawn- 74. Round cream filled cookie 75. Mexican moolah- 76. Relax- 77. Go ___ (small racer)- 78. Had a bite

Down

1. Grows weary- 2. Intelligent- 3. Understanding- 4. Hindu garment 5. Gradually withdraw- 6. Onassis nickname- 7. Secret Chinese society 8. Photo or record- 9. Either or neither ___ - 10. Honk- 11. Apple gizmo- 12. Ceramic floor square- 15. QB's gains (abbr)- 20. What you do with eyes- 22. Not used- 25. Not the beginning- 27. Mao ___ tung- 29. Peak: uppermost- 30. Apprehend- 31. "___ Karenina" 33. Allergic reaction- 34. Miami ___ County- 35. Besides instead 36. Pass as time- 37. Hot and dry- 38. Necessity- 40. Cookware 44. Have a go at- 47. Tint- 49. Ancient mummy king- 51. Large coffee dispenser- 53. Sugary suffix- 55. Pigeon's perch- 57. Quartet doubled 58. Actress Witherspoon- 59. Note from the boss- 60. Baby food catcher 61. Stench- 62. Suffix for hard or soft- 64. "Return of the Jedi" creature 65. prophet- 66. Cold annoyance- 69. Fellows- 71. Memorable period of time- 72. Health retreat

5 Take a careful look at these two sets of characters. Which characters appear in the series on the right but not in the series on the left?

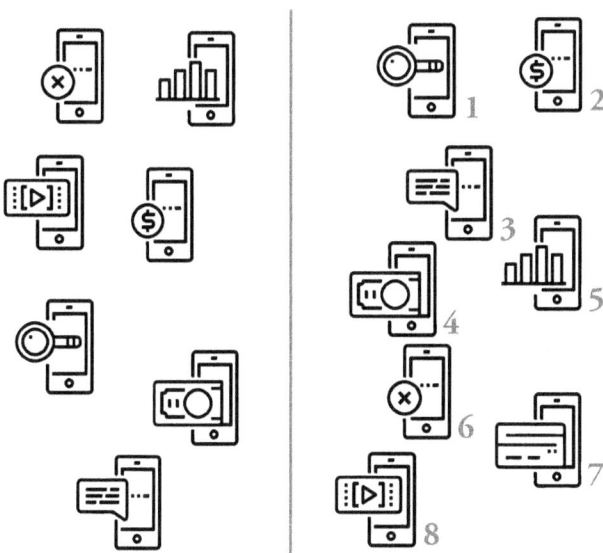

6 Try to solve the below Sudoku puzzle and note that each row, column, and nonet (sections of nine bordered cells) can contain each number (typically 1 to 9) exactly once

9			6		2	7		4
3				8	5			9
	5	7	4					6
7		2			6	9		
	9	6	1	2	3	8	7	
		5	9			2		1
1		3			8	4	9	
6			2	7				8
5		8				6		2

7 Determine the fewest number of moves necessary to change the configuration in Figure A to that shown in Figure B. You may not place a larger disk on a smaller one, and you may move only one disk at a time.

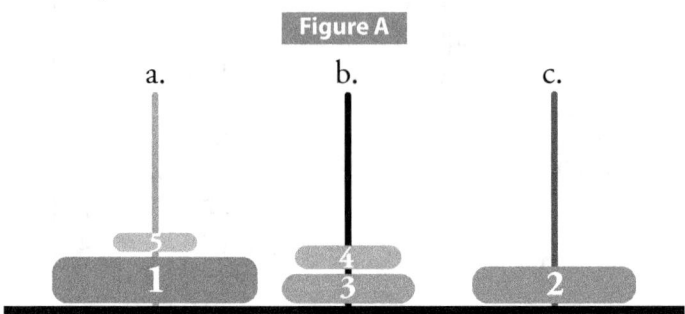

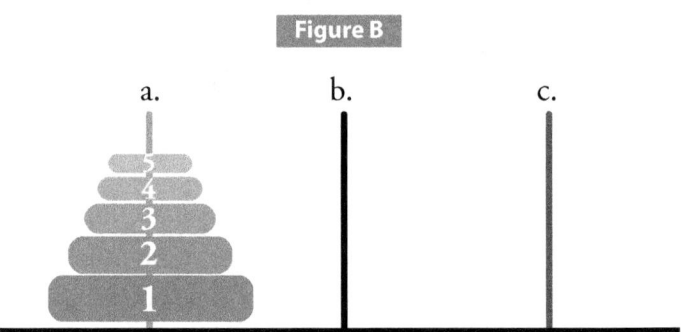

Number of movements:

8 Which picture should replace the question marks?

Part 1

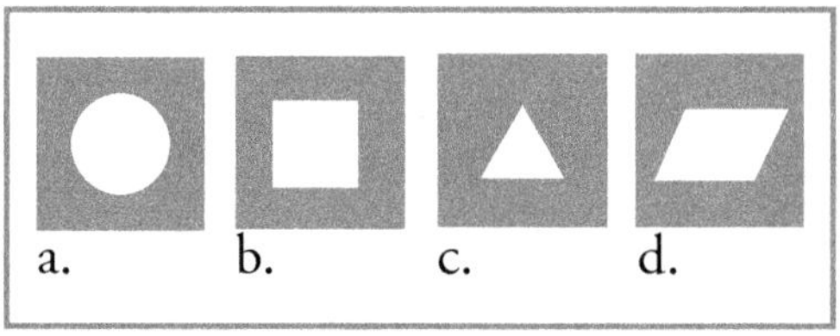

a. b. c. d.

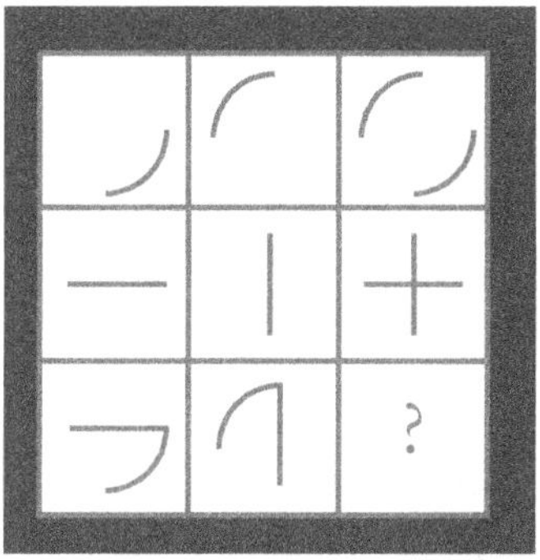

Part 2

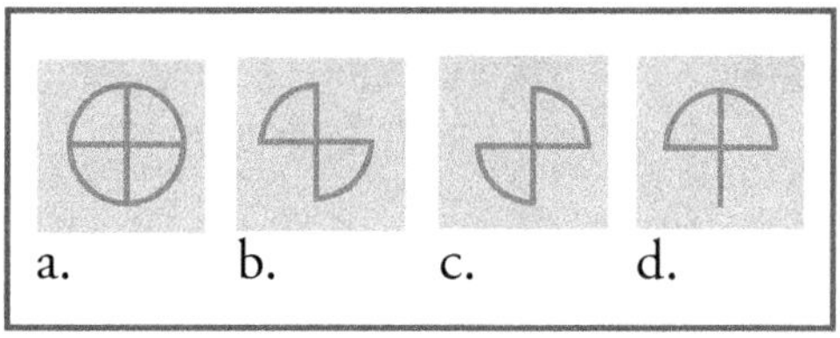

a. b. c. d.

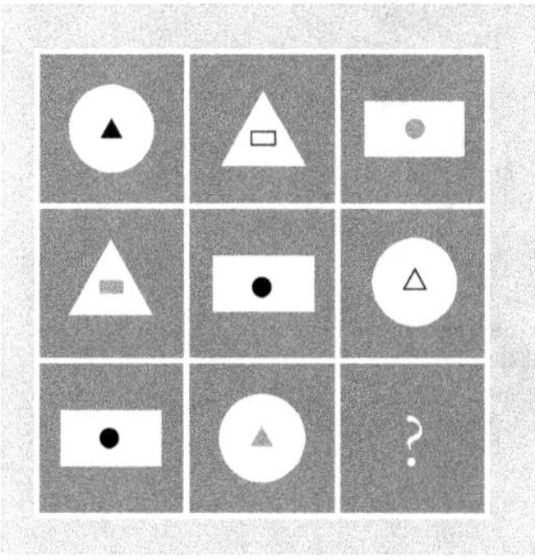

Part 3

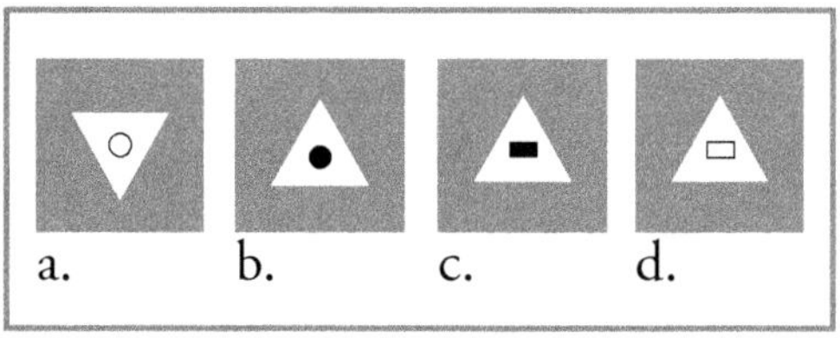

a. b. c. d.

9 Draw the picture, in place of the question mark.

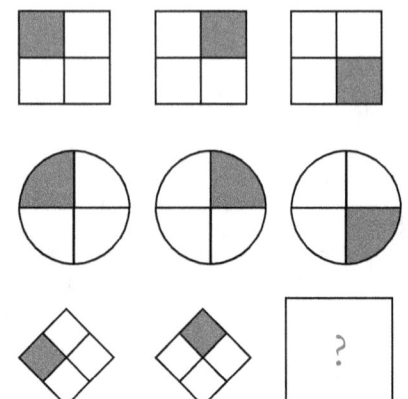

 10 Draw the other half of the picture.

Report Card

Date   Number of incorrect answers   Time duration
Main weak points

Conclusion

Brain Club
10th Session

 **Brain Education**

1 How might my restored brain functions help me to revive my family life during recovery?

Being in a supportive family and receiving help from family members in different phases of the rehabilitation process could help speed-up your brain recovery. Having meaningful social interactions with family and letting them be participants in the process of your recovery, alongside you, can make a positive effect on treatment outcomes. After you re-achieve your brain functions, you can play a more effective role in your family in terms of improving relationships and accepting more responsibility.

2 Does my addiction recovery depend upon having a powerful brain?

Drug addiction is associated with a lack of inhibitory power in your brain. As much as your brain loses its functioning power, it becomes more difficult to cope with the urge of drug use (triggers and craving) and decreases your ability to make proper decisions. You need a healthy brain to navigate the treatment process. With an increasingly powerful brain you can learn treatment materials (e.g., compensatory and coping strategies) transferred during therapeutic sessions and apply them in everyday life.

Brain Exercises (Main Session)

 1 All the ladybugs except one are repeated three times. Find the single one.

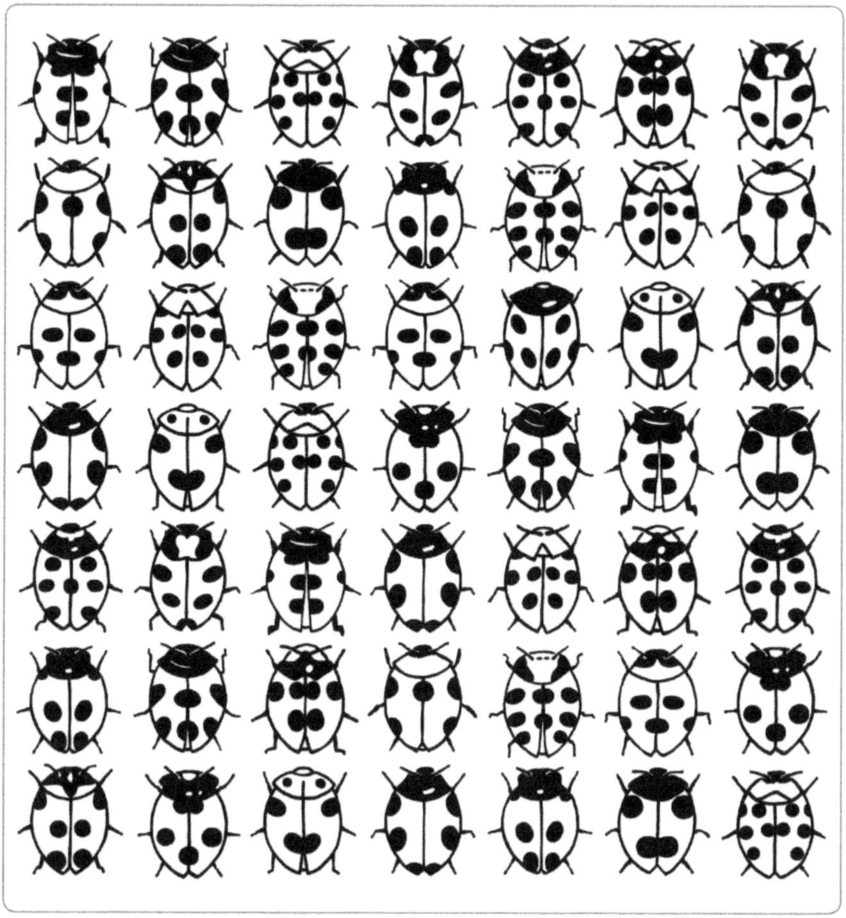

2 In this exercise, you can see different boxes written with one direction (left, right, up, down). For the first part of exercise, read just the direction but for the second part accurately name the direction according to where they have been written in the box. Record your time for both parts and compare them.

Part 1: Direction

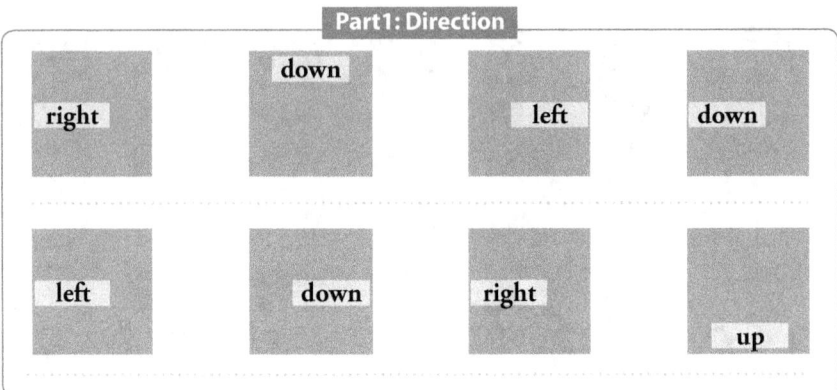

Time (sec): _____   Number of errors: _____

Part 2: Location of direction with regard to square

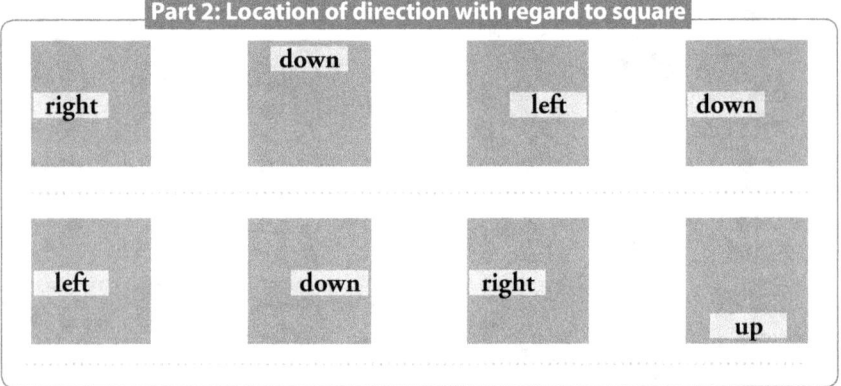

Time (sec): _____   Number of errors: _____

3 What number should replace the question mark?

2	1	1	2
3	1	2	2
1	3	2	4
4	1	2	?

4 Look at the faces below and try to identify the emotion conveyed in each face.

① ② ③ ④ ⑤

 5 Scan the below images and try to find as many as target pictures and write the total number and mark them as identifed for each target picture.

Total number: ...... Total number: ...... Total number: ......
Total number: ......

6 Look carefully at the following pairs of images and try to spot differences.

7 differences

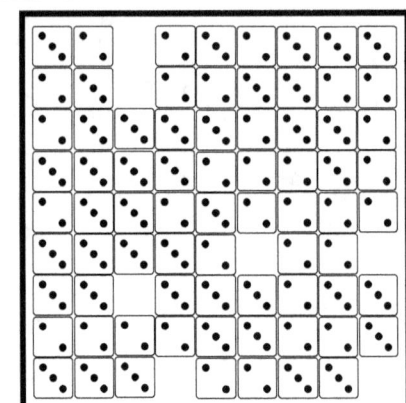

 7 Draw the other half of the picture.

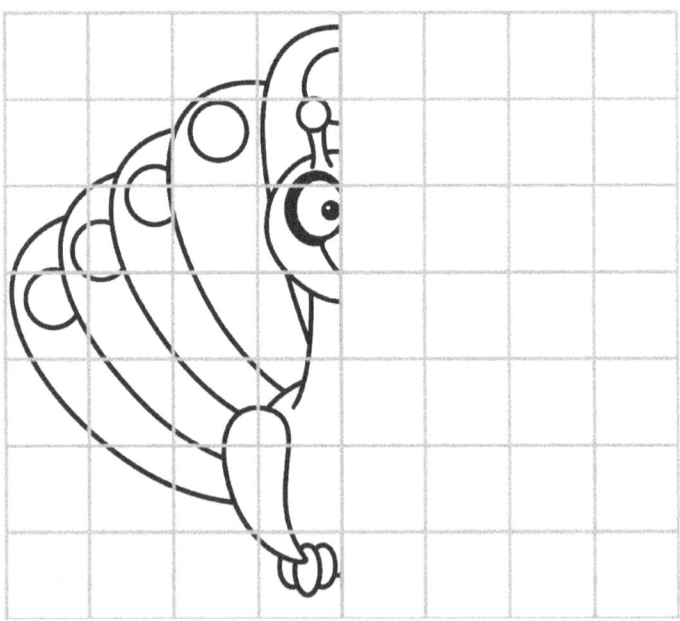

8 Calculate each series of numbers based on the specified order and write the final answer.

Add	12	7	3	5	10	20	11	4	?
Add	19	5	7	1	8	31	2	7	?
Subtract	120	5	10	9	4	14	5	41	?
Add	6	21	14	8	11	3	15	10	?
Multiply	4	2	3	2	1	3	2	2	?
Subtract	420	30	21	10	3	17	9	60	?
Subtract	240	20	17	3	16	8	21	6	?
Multiply	5	2	4	3	2	3	1	2	?
Multiply	2	2	3	4	2	3	2	1	?
Add	12	10	5	7	8	9	7	3	?
Add	36	5	7	8	6	7	6	10	?
Add	21	4	11	6	4	19	5	8	?
Subtract	180	21	7	11	7	5	8	7	?
Multiply	3	2	2	3	2	4	1	2	?
Subtract	370	52	16	7	5	8	11	20	?

9 Complete the cross-table with numbers 1 to 10.

1	×		+	5	=	8
+		×		+		
	×	4	×		=	48
+		+		×		
	+		+		=	24
=		=		=		
14		20		63		

10 Use each of the following numbers and equations once to reach the determined answer.

a. 1, 2, 3, 5, 7   +, -, ×, ×   ➤ 43
b. 2, 2, 5, 7, 25   +, +, ×, ×   ➤ 117
c. 1, 2, 3, 7, 25, 100   +, -, -, ×, ×   ➤ 619
d. 4, 4, 5, 6, 8, 75   +, +, ×, ×, ÷   ➤ 255

a. **43 =**
b. **117 =**
c. **619 =**
d. **255 =**

11 What numbers should replace the blank spaces?

	3	4	6	9
			9	12
	8	9		14
	9	10	12	

a. 6 8 / 12 / 15   b. 6 7 / 11 / 15   c. 5 7 / 11 / 15   d. 5 8 / 12 / 16

12 Look carefully at the following pair of images and try to spot differences.

10 differences

Date   Number of incorrect answers   Time duration

Main weak points

Conclusion

Report Card

Extra Exercises (Home-work)

 ❶ See the below picture and try to find all of the chickens.

22 chickens

2 In this exercise, you can see different boxes including one of four directions(left, right, up, down). For the first part of exercise, read just the direction but for the second part accurately name the direction according to where they have been written in the box. Record your time for both parts and compare them.

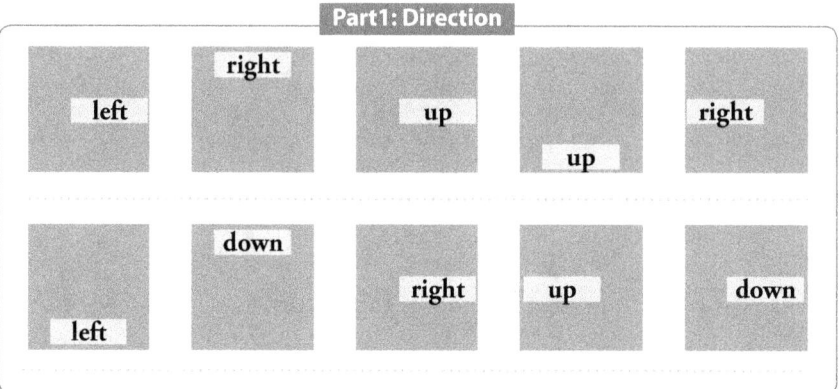

Time (sec): _____   Number of errors: _____

Time (sec): _____   Number of errors: _____

3 What image should replace the question mark?

4 Find the different one in this series.

5 What image should replace the blank space?

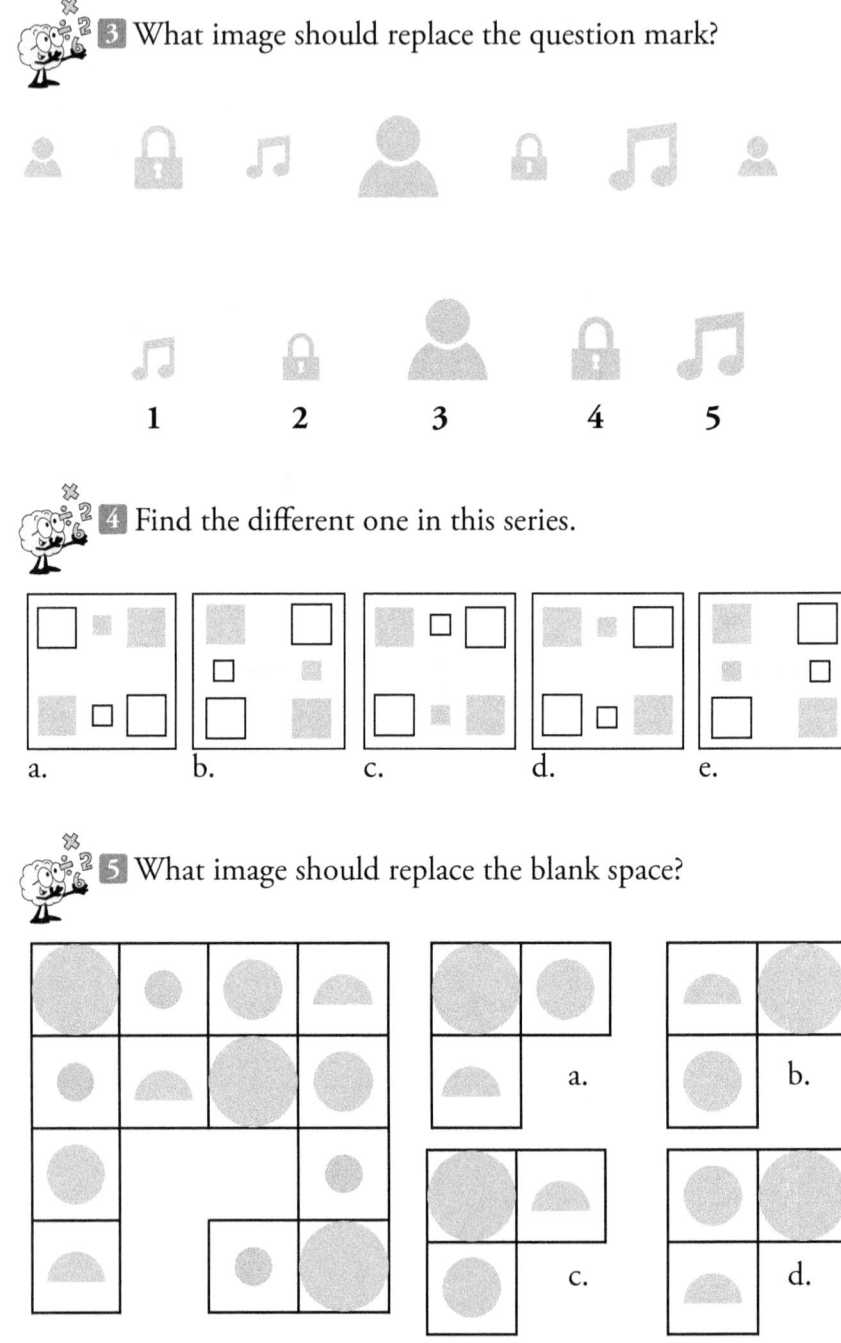

6 Look at the faces below and try to identify the emotion conveyed in each face.

7 Scan the below images and try to find as many as target pictures and write the total number and mark them as identified.

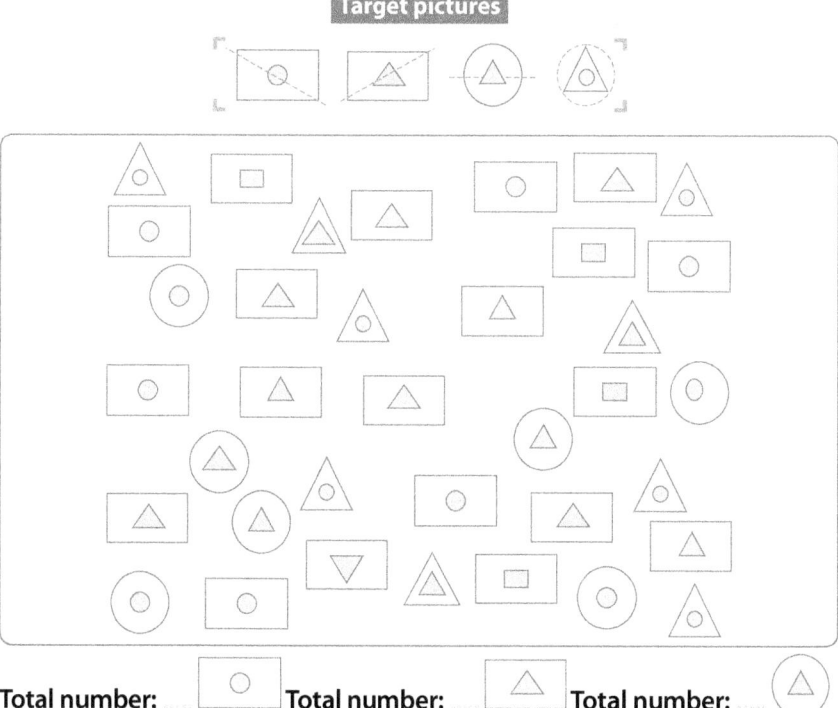

Total number: _____   Total number: _____   Total number: _____
Total number: _____

 8 Look carefully at the following pair of images and try to spot differences.

20 differences

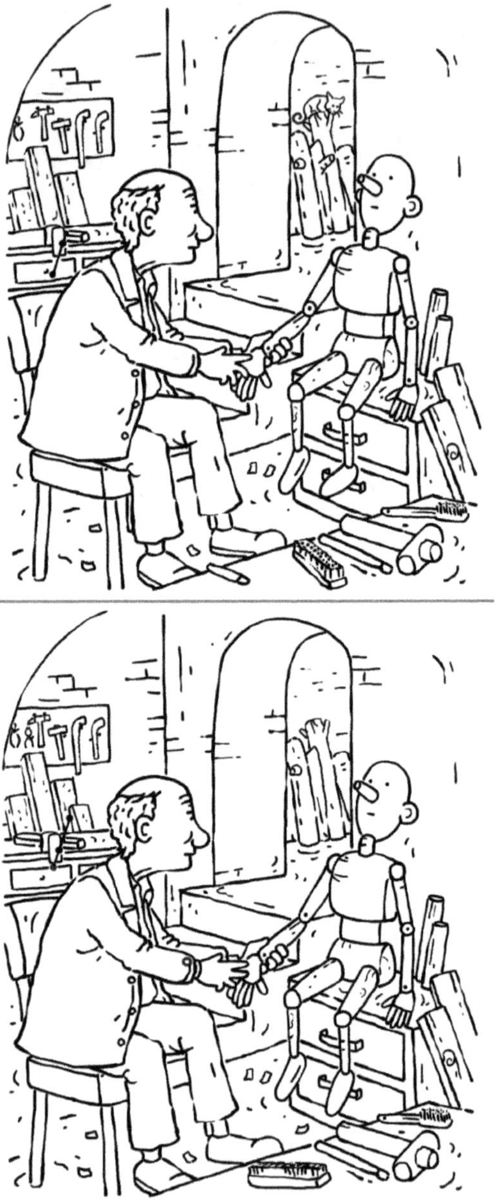

9 Complete the cross-table with numbers.

3	×		−		=	16
×		×		×		
	÷	1	×		=	8
×		+		+		
	×		+	8	=	62
=		=		=		
72		16		18		

 10 What number should replace the question mark to continue the sequence?
a. 1, 3, 7, 15, 31, 63, ?
b. 4, 4, 6, 12, 30, 90, ?
c. 3, 5, 10, 12, 24, 26, ?

 11 See the below picture and try to find all of the coil.

15 coils

12 What numbers should replace the blank spaces in the below cross-table?

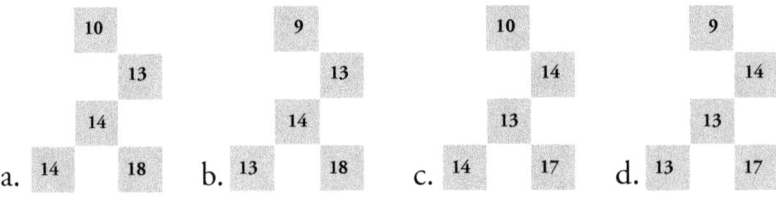

a.   b.   c.   d.

 13 What number should replace the question mark?

5	8	2	3
2	7	6	5
9	1	7	1
4	2	5	?

Date   **Number of incorrect answers**   **Time duration**

Main weak points

Conclusion

Brain Club
11th Session

Brain Education

1 When is a good time to start "Brain Trainings" after initial detoxification and/or early abstinence?

As much as you need to do some controlled physical exercises after you remove a cast from a healing arm to regain muscle strength, your brain's muscle needs exercises to re-achieve its lost power. But the main point here is the level of difficulty of exercises should be adjusted carefully by your therapist/counselor. These moderate exercises can not only activate your brain but also prevents excessive stress due to rigorous exercises that may be not very helpful for your healing brain.

2 Do I need a coach for brain training?

An expert counselor or therapist can help you as your brain trainer or coach in the process of rehabilitation of brain functions. The coach can support your recovery process by applying properly adjusted exercises and teaching useful and practical strategies that are necessary for speeding up the recovery. The coach can design a customized rehabilitation program to meet your brain's needs. For example, if your attention is impaired more than memory, your coach can use a program more designed toward attention training and related skills. But even if you do not have access to an expert, you may still use regular daily brain exercises in your routine schedule and see its benefits.

Brain Exercises (Main Session)

1 Read the below paragraphs and find the letters specified for each part. Note that you should find the letters simultaneously.

Letters "T/t", "Y/y", "O/o"

The health benefits of copper include proper growth of the body, efficient utilization of iron, proper enzymatic reactions, as well as improved health of connective tissues, hair, and eyes. It is also integral for preventing premature aging and increasing energy production. Apart from these, regulated heart rhythm, balanced thyroid glands, reduced symptoms of arthritis, quick wound healing, increased red blood cell formation, and reduced cholesterol are other health benefits of copper. The health benefits of copper are crucial for an overall healthy existence, as this mineral enables normal metabolic process in association with amino acids and vitamins. It cannot be produced within the body and therefore needs to be added from external food sources. It is the third most prevalent mineral in the body and it is mostly carried by the blood plasma protein, Ceruloplasmin. In order to enjoy the health benefits of copper, it must be included in the daily diet, as it is used up in daily bodily processes. Copper is present in various food sources including liver, meat, seafood, beans, whole grains, soy flour, wheat bran, almonds, avocados, barley, garlic, nuts, oats, blackstrap molasses, beets and lentils. It also enters the human body through drinking water in copper pipes and by using copper cookware.

Number of letters "T/t", "Y/y", "O/o": ....

2 Link the upward arrows and downward arrows consecutively, without raising your pencil. Note that you can not touch other arrows and you can not pass through each specified arrow more than once.

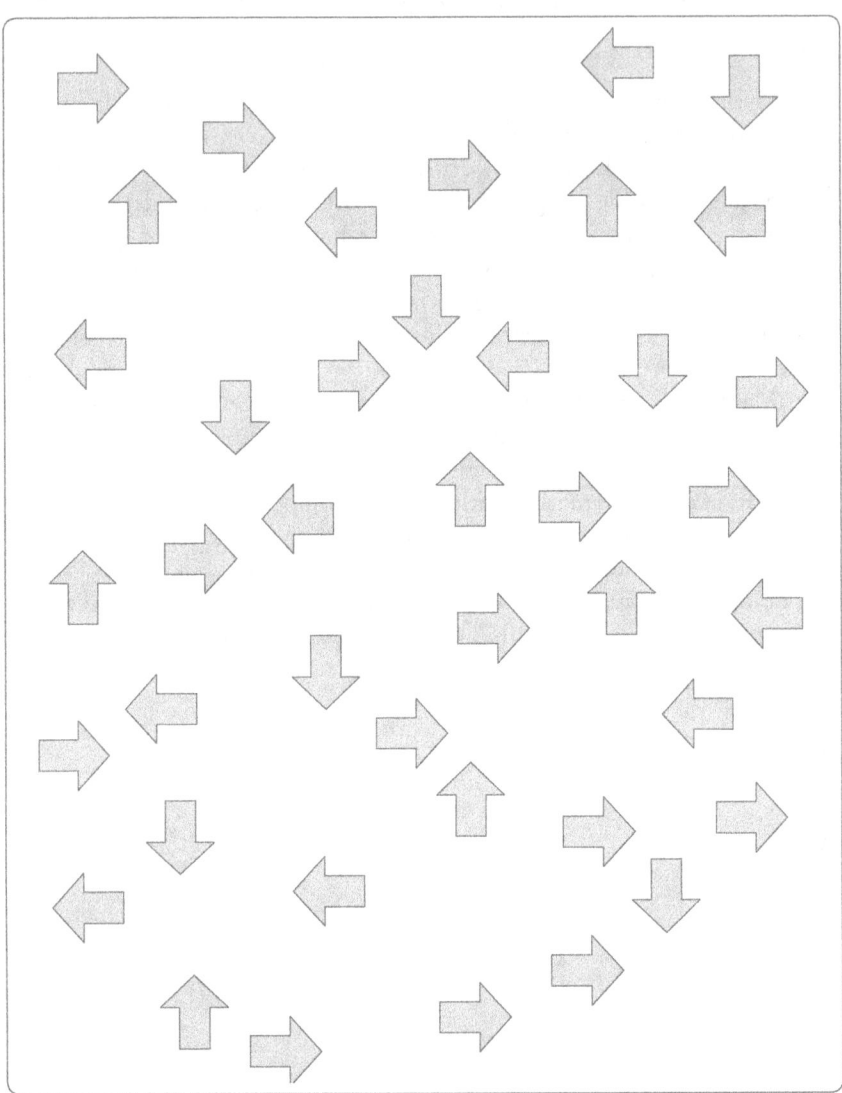

Time (sec):

3 Try to find a path between the gray and pink arrows that joins the entrance and the exit parts of the path.

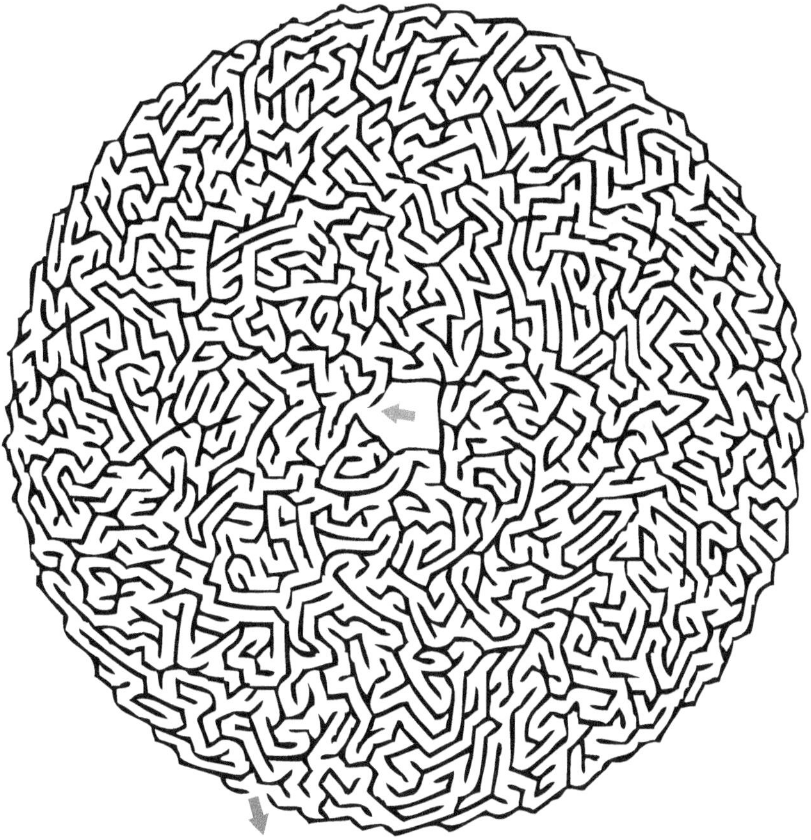

4 Find the odd one in this series.

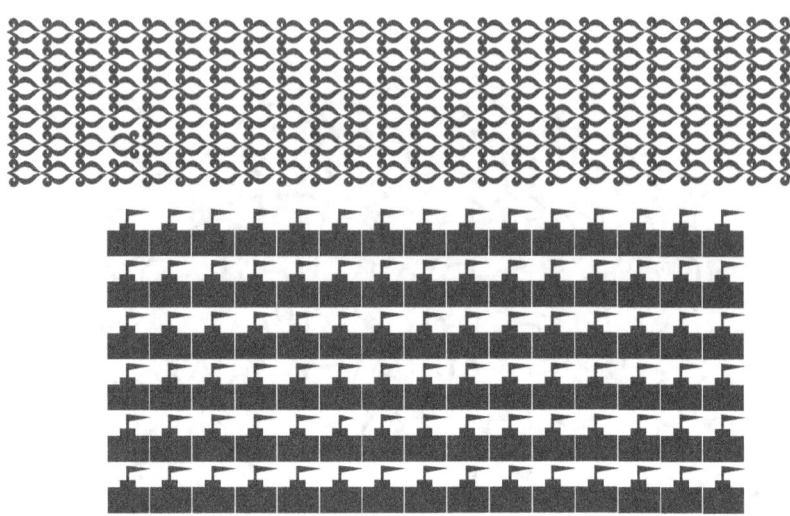

 5 Try to find the identical pair.

6 See the figure below; then determine which three of the nine figures below are combined to form the main figure.

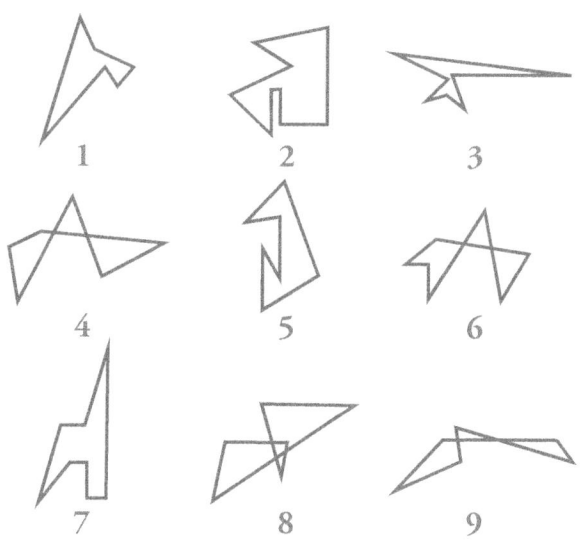

7 Which of the three tiles below completes the picture?

a. b. c.

 8 How many triangles and rectangles are in this picture?

Number of rectangles: ....
Number of triangles: ....

9 For each of the three pictures on the left, which of the images on the right would result from rotating the picture in the way shown by the arrow (90 degrees counter-clockwise, 180 degrees and 90 degrees clockwise respectively)?

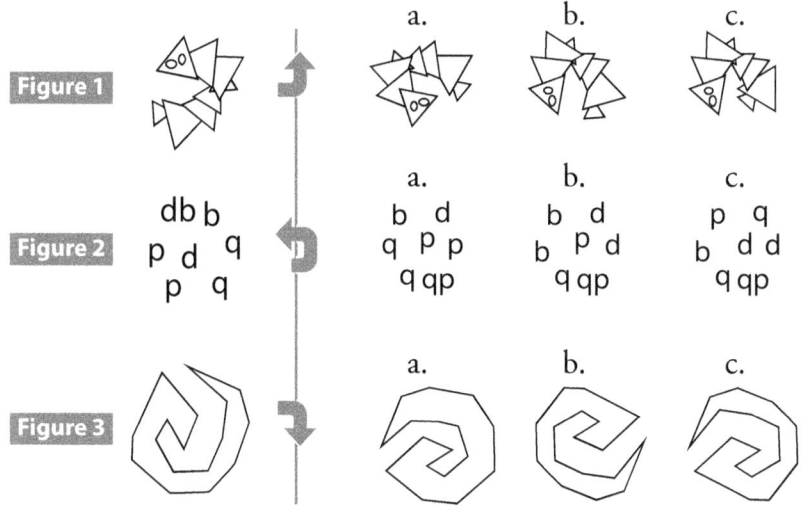

10 How many triangles are in this picture?

Number of triangles: _____

Date   Number of incorrect answers   Time duration
Main weak points

Conclusion

Extra Exercises (Home-work)

1 Read the below paragraphs and find the letters specified for each part. Note that you should find the letters simultaneously.

Letters "V/v", "S/s", "H/h"

The domestic cat is a small, typically furry, carnivorous mammal. They are often called house cats when kept as indoor pets or simply cats when there is no need to distinguish them from other felids and felines. Cats are often valued by humans for companionship and for their ability to hunt vermin. There are more than 70 cat breeds, though different associations proclaim different numbers according to their standards. Cats are similar in anatomy to the other felids, with a strong flexible body, quick reflexes, sharp retractable claws, and teeth adapted to killing small prey. Cat senses fit a crepuscular and predatory ecological niche. Cats can hear sounds too faint or too high in frequency for human ears, such as those made by mice and other small animals. They can see in near darkness. Like most other mammals, cats have poorer color vision and a better sense of smell than humans. Cats, despite being solitary hunters, are a social species and cat communication includes the use of a variety of vocalizations, as well as cat pheromones and types of cat-specific body language. Cats have a high breeding rate. Under controlled breeding, they can be bred and shown as registered pedigree pets, a hobby known as cat fancy. Failure to control the breeding of pet cats by neutering, as well as the abandonment of former household pets, has resulted in large numbers of feral cats worldwide, requiring population control. In certain areas outside cats' native range, this has contributed, along with habitat destruction and other factors, to the extinction of many bird species. Cats have been known to extirpate a bird species within specific regions and may have contributed to the extinction of isolated island populations. Cats are thought to be primarily responsible for the extinction of 33 species of birds, and the presence of feral and free-ranging cats makes some otherwise suitable locations unsuitable for attempted species reintroduction.

Number of letters "V/v", "S/s", "H/h": ....

2 Link the left directed arrows and right directed arrows consecutively, without raising your pencil. Note that you can not touch other arrows and you can not pass through each specified arrow more than once.

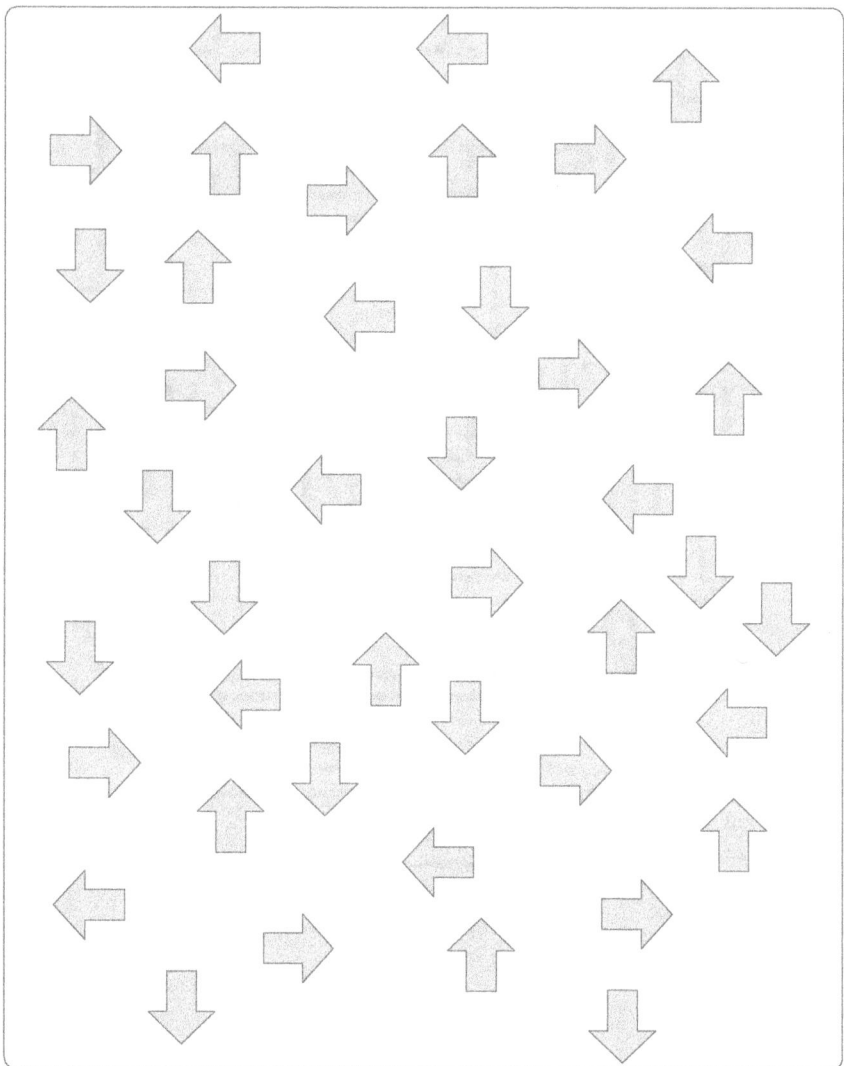

Time (sec):

 3 Try to find a path between the gray and pink arrows that joins the entrance and the exit parts of the path.

4 Try to find the the identical pair.

 5 Find the odd one in this series.

6 Below are pictures of three objects overlapping each other. Try to figure out what each of the images are.

Figure 1

Figure 2

Figure 3

Figure 4

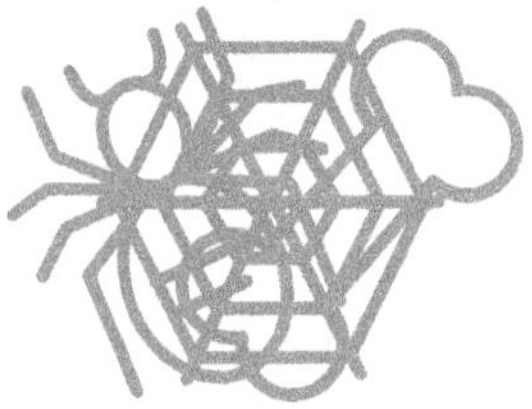

Figure 1:

Figure 2:

Figure 3:

Figure 4:

7 Among the hands below, find the right hands and the left hands.

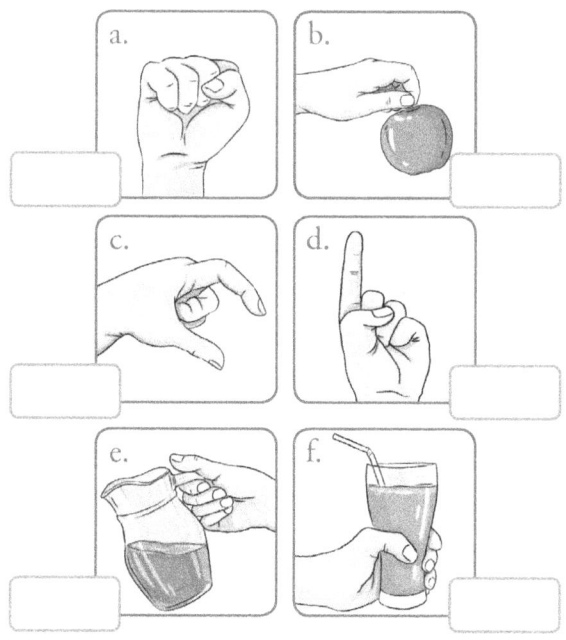

 8 How many triangles are in this picture?

Number of triangles: _____

9 Try to find all hidden items in the picture and circle them.

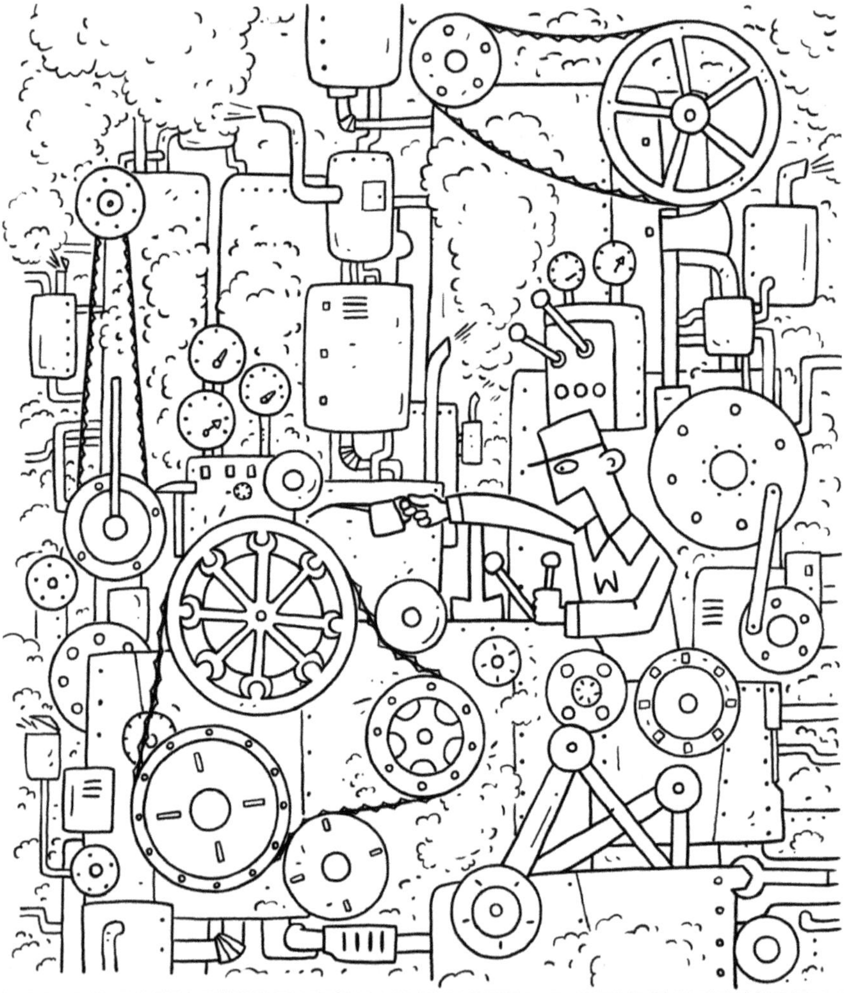

Report Card	**Date**	**Number of incorrect answers**	**Time duration**
	Main weak points		
	Conclusion		

Brain Club
12th Session

Brain Education

1 How many times per day I should do brain exercises?

The two most important issues in regard to brain exercises are the frequency and the intensity of exercises you do in a daily routine. Remember that your brain is in the healing process and any excessive stress could reduce the speed of recovery and cause problems such as fatigue and tension. So, you need to be careful about the intensity of exercises. If you have brain trainer coach, he/she can monitor this procedure and tune up the intensity and frequency of prescribed training schedule that are customized for you. But, if you do not have a brain coach, we recommend you to do brain exercises as part of a daily routine (3 days per week as a minimum) for 30-45 minutes with intensity that creates enough mental pressure without adding undue emotional stress.

2 How can I make myself committed to do my exercises?

The first asset in committing to something like regularly doing brain exercises, could be internal incentive. You can encourage yourself by positive internal dialogue or determining a reward for yourself. For example, after each time you complete your daily exercise, you can do one of your favorite activities or treating yourself by buying something that motivates you for the remaining parts of program. Keeping track of your activities by writing-down the time you invested every day and itemizing your achievements could enhance your motivation.

Brain Exercises (Main Session)

 1 Write a paragraph with the below words and use each of them only once.

> kitchen, car, repair, water, neighbor, sunny, children

 **2** Complete the following sayings.

a. A golden ...... can ...... any door
b. A journey of a ...... miles begins with a ......
c. A person is ...... by the ...... he keeps
d. After a storm ......
e. All good things must ......

 3 In the exercise, you can see 12 paired words. read them for 30 seconds and then go to the next page.

camera boat	chain mouse	church beach	pot library	rabbit clock	wheel warehouse
towel wallpaper	chimney hotel	hand elephant	rope bowl	telephone Paris	newspaper river

12th step | 187

Without returning to the previous page, try to identify the paired words you have read.

camera, church, telephone, pot, rabbit, mouse, clock, wheel, boat, chain, river, elephant, chimney, hotel, warehouse, beach, wallpaper, library, towel, Paris, bowl, newspaper, hand, rope

  4 Use association to get from the first word to the last one to make a logical order to make a meaningful sequence. Write the appropriate word for each space.

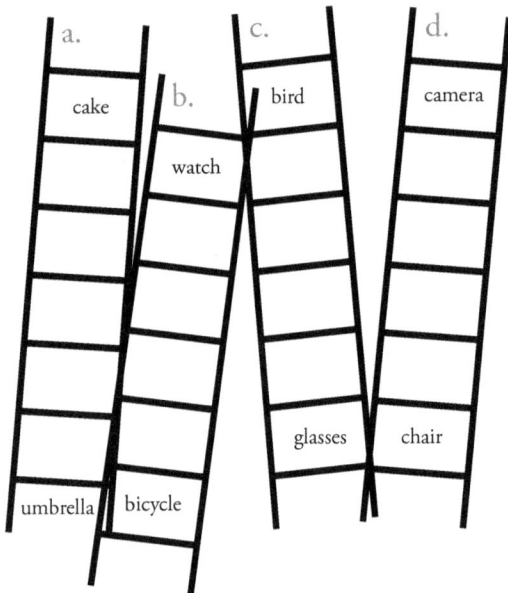

5 Take a careful look at these two sets of characters. Which characters appear in the series on the right but not in the series on the left?

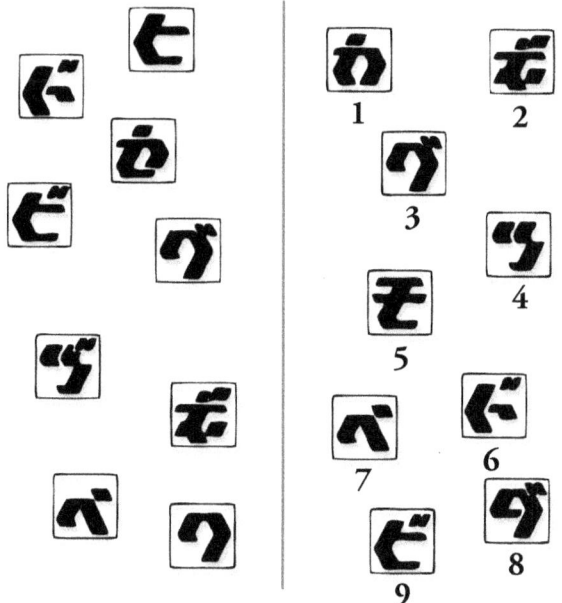

 6 Try to find the logical order of the below pictures.

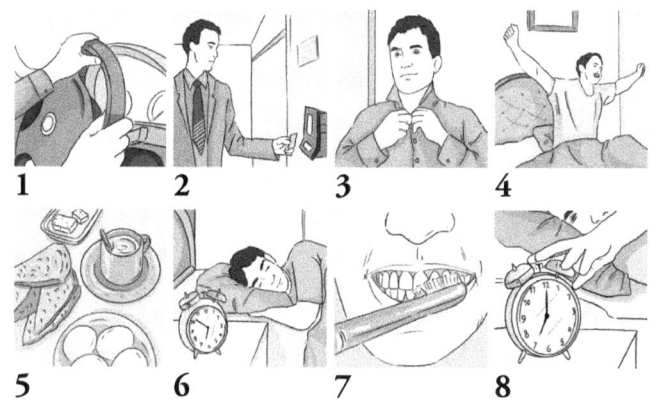

The right sequence of pictures (from left to right):

7 Try to solve the below Sudoku puzzle and note that each row, column, and nonet (sections of nine bordered cells) can contain each number (typically 1 to 9) exactly once

1			5					8
	8		3			5	6	9
	7				2	1		3
		7		3				6
8			1		6			2
6				5		9		
7		9	4					5
5	4	6		9			3	
	2				5			1

 8 Look at the below faces for 5 seconds and then turn to the next page.

Without turning to the previous page, try to redraw the four faces as precisely as possible.

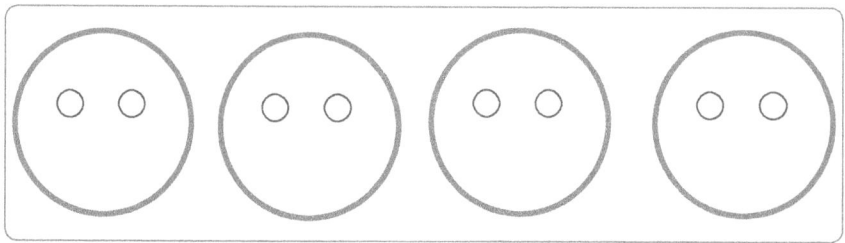

9 Determine the fewest number of moves necessary to change the configuration in Figure A to that shown in Figure B. You may not place a larger disk on a smaller one, and you may move only one disk at a time.

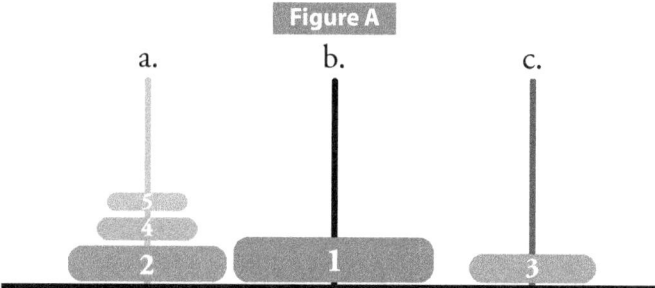

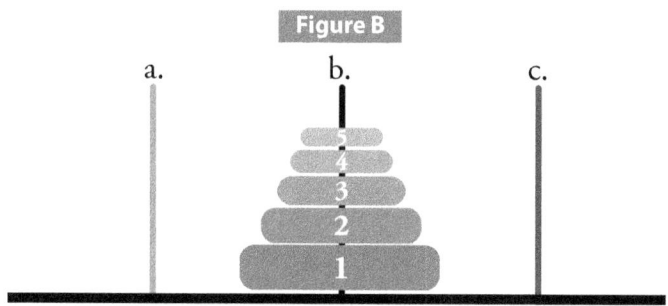

Number of movements:

10 Try to complete the below cross-word.

Across

1. "___ Miz"- 4. Close a door loudly- 8. Skyrocket- 12. Ready and willing- 13. Fiddling emperor- 14. Eagle's claw- 16. Pronto- 17.Gets older- 18. Fiery felony- 19. Pressure unit- 20. A long time ___ - 21. Child's game- 23. Words of praise- 24. Kind of eclipse 26. Homer's neighbor- 28. "___ a Wonderfull Life"- 30. Yank- 32. Deli loaves 36. Student residence- 39. Thirst quenchers- 41. Kennel cry- 42. Lincoln or Vigoda 43. Want too much- 45. Tell an untruth- 46. Christmastime- 48. Take apart- 49. Escaped 50. Snakelike fish- 51. Abdominal muscles- 52. See you later- 54. Had done- 56. Outer limits- 60. Actor Wallach- 63. May Honoree- 65. Ltr add-ons- 67. Phase of sleep- 68. Great enthusiasm- 70. Spoken- 72. Lima's country- 73. Big band music- 74. Dash- 75. Reagan secretary of state- 76. Rational- 77. Spotted- 78. Native: suffix

Down

1. Cowboy's rope- 2. In-box filler- 3. Fall mo- 4. Capture- 5. Building block brand 6. He is, we ___ - 7. Majority- 8.Theater section- 9. Canoe paddle- 10. Too- 11. Large cross- 12. Voids- 15. SSW opposite- 20. Wall hanging- 22. Director Lee- 25. Target towards a goal- 27. Boring- 29. Hang loosely- 30. Adolescents- 31. Secondhand- 33. Holler- 34. Novelist Wiesel- 35. Past of speed- 36. Great ___ dog- 37. Bassoon cousin- 38. Rod and ___ - 40. Defeat soundly- 44. ID datum, briefly 47. Psychedelic drug- 49. Supplied food- 51. Ruckus- 53. Affirmative- 55. Appearance- 57. Extraordinary- 58. Spooky- 59. Overcenfident- 60. Type measures- 61. Attorney's expertise- 62. Dolphin genus- 64. A bit extra- 65. Walk back and forth- 66. Toboggan 69. Hostel- 71. Barb-tailed fish- 72. Greek letter

11 What picture should replace the question mark?

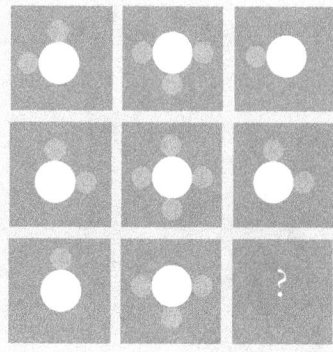

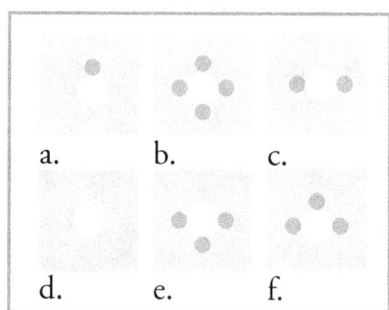

a. b. c.

d. e. f.

 12 What would be the rotated image of below image?

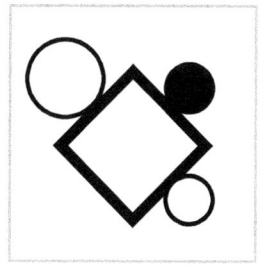

a.

b.

c.

Date   **Number of incorrect answers**   **Time duration**
Main weak points

Conclusion

⚡ Extra Exercises (Home-work)

 1 Write one paragraph about the below image in 4 minutes.

....
....

 2 Try to remind below names and their job for 45 seconds, then go to the next page.

Names	Jobs
David Jonson	Farmer
Ben Connel	Chef
Sara Baxter	Nurse
Lee Montgomery	Driver
Jack Hopkins	Baker
Ariel Rabin	Teacher
Sharon Barak	Mechanics

Without returning to the previous page, fill the gaps with last names and jobs related to each name.
Last name: Jonson,Connel,Baxter,Montgomery,Hopkins,Rabin,Barak
Jobs: driver, mechanics, baker, nurse, farmer, chef, teacher

Names	Last name	Job
David		
Ben		
Sara		
Lee		
Jack		
Ariel		
Sharon		

 3 Complete the following sayings.

a. .... **lead to Rome**
b. **Ask a** .... **question and you'll** .... **a silly** ....
c. **Behind** .... **man there's a** .... **woman**
d. **Don't cast your** .... **before** ....
e. **Don't cross the** .... **till you come** ....

 4 Look at the pictures below for 15 seconds and then turn to the next page.

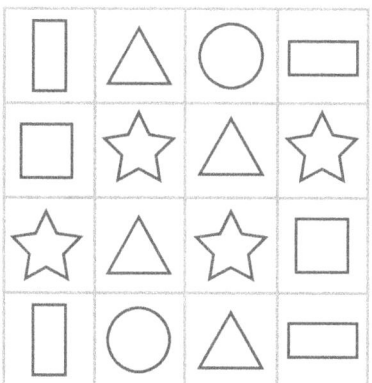

12th step | 195

Without returning to the previous page, try to draw image you have seen in previous page.

5 Take a careful look at these two sets of characters. Which characters appear in the series on the right but not in the series on the left?

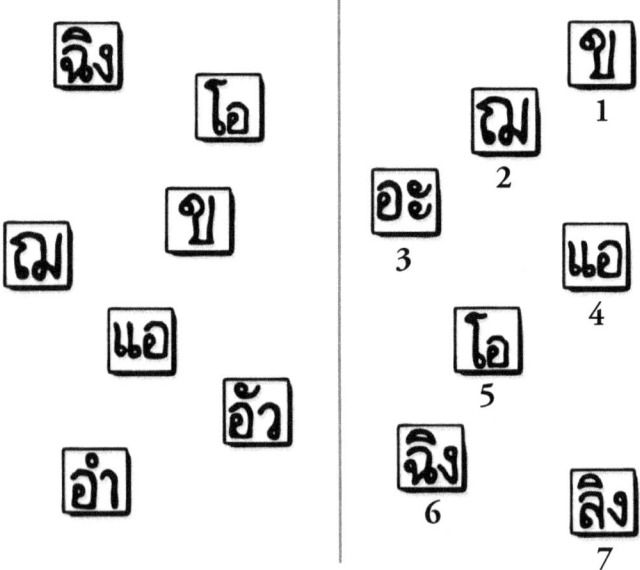

6 Use association to get from the first word to the last one to make a logical order to make a meaningful sequence. Write the appropriate word for each space.

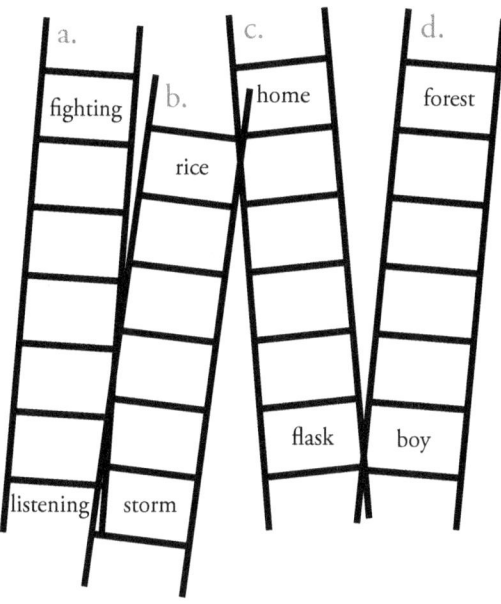

7 Try to solve the below Sudoku puzzle and note that each row, column, and nonet (sections of nine bordered cells) can contain each number (typically 1 to 9) exactly once.

				5		2		
6		5						
		7	3		6		9	
					2		8	9
2			8		4			7
3	7		6					2
	8		7		1	5		
1			9			8		
			6		4			1

8 Try to complete the below cross-word.

Across

1. Part of WWII- 4. Spanish house- 8. Mouth off- 12. Weeps loudly- 13. Pub orders 14. Shipping container- 16. Speed between walk and run- 17. Security device 18. Buyer's proposal- 19. Ohio State University (abbr)- 20. Frequently- 21. Farm female- 23. Female sheep- 24. Room up top- 26. Yankovic and Pacino- 28. Had a snack- 30. Not in operation- 32. Once ____ a time- 36. Gramp's wife- 39. Speak unclearly- 41. Detective Wolfe- 42. Feel poorly- 43. Doctrine- 45. Green prefix 46. Falcon feature- 48. Breezes through- 49. Muffin choice- 50. Movie lioness 51. Put to work- 52. Australian bird- 54. Humped wild ox of Asia- 56. Burger topper 60. Receding tide- 63. H.S proficiency test- 65. Arrow launcher- 67. Baseball scoreboard trio- 68. Less common- 70. Made a perfect serve- 72. Very narrow shoe width- 73. Blinding light- 74. Garden intruder- 75. Computer key- 76. A ____ formality- 77. Goalies quard them- 78. A hot drink

Down

1. Baddest- 2. Regarding- 3. Alphabet sequence- 4. Farm newborn- 5. Oodles , 2 wds 6. 1/60 min- 7. Poses questions- 8. Angry look- 9. Dog sound- 10. Place to leave valuables- 11. One-pot dinner- 12. Greek colonnade- 15. Before in verse- 20. Halloween mo- 22. A dolt- 25. James Bond creator Fleming- 27. Closest star- 29. Superlative suffix 30. Small weight- 31. At no charge- 33. Look intently- 34. Ocean predator- 35. 12:00 36. Comedian Kaplan- 37. Cambodian currency- 38. Distressed sigh- 40. Meadows 44. Mao ____ tung- 47. Mary ____ cosmetics- 49. Burger container- 51. Ukulele (abbr) 53. Tend the lawn- 55. Concur- 57. Very angry- 58. Scarlett of "Gone With The Wind"- 59. Oscar winner Patricia- 60. Unit of force- 61. Ointment- 62. Highland hillside- 64. First light- 65. Shade of red- 66. Likelihood- 69. Mess up- 71. Mediocre grade- 72. Part of a play

9 What picture should replace the question marks?

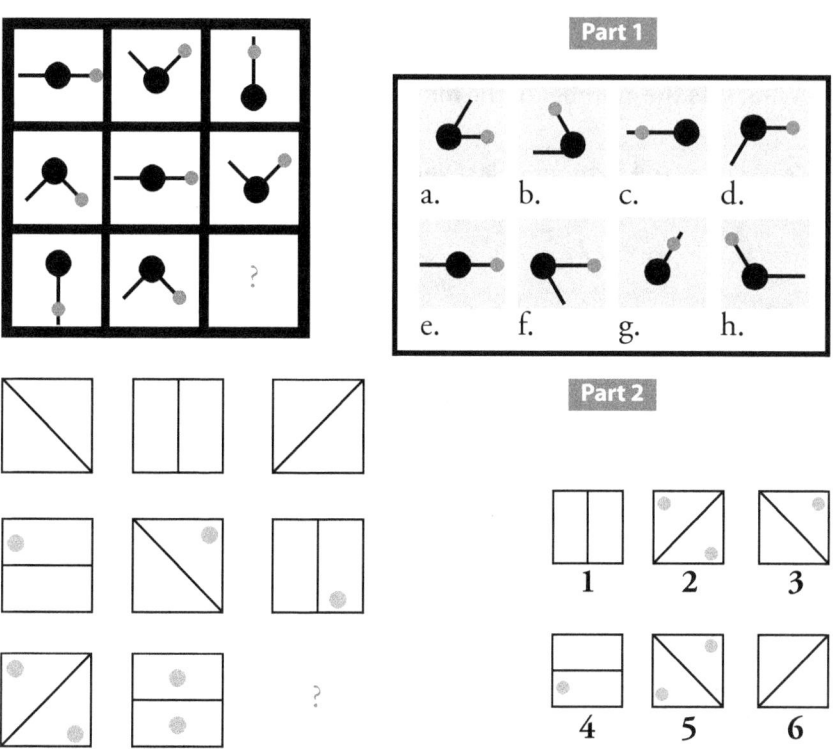

10 Look at the below image and try to remember the color and number of each shirt for 15 seconds and then go to the next page.

a. What was the sum of all even numbers?

b. What was the sum of all odd numbers?

c. What was the number of the middle player?

d. What were the number of last and first players?

11 What picture should replace the question mark?

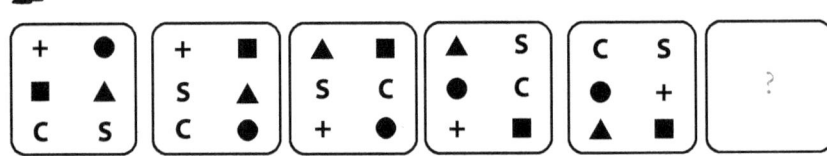

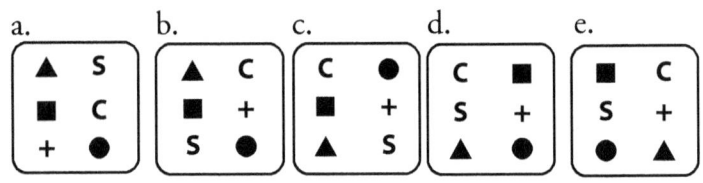

Date   Number of incorrect answers   Time duration
Main weak points

Conclusion

Report Card

Brain Club
13th Session

 Brain Education

1 Does daily work in my job or studies act as "brain exercise"?
As we have mentioned before, we need our brain functions for every task we do in every day life even for the simplest ones such as choosing proper clothes for a meeting, preparing dinner and driving in a familiar place (and so-on). So, our daily activities, especially those which require more attention and concentration, could act as a brain exercise. But, they cannot substitute for active brain trainings designed to systematically engage different brain functions with upgraded intensity over time.

2 Is there any limitation for the pressure I would apply to my brain with exercises?
Too much pressure, especially when you are doing complicated and difficult exercises, could slow your brain functions and reduce your power to concentrate. So, it is important to allow your "coach" to help adjust the level of brain exercises that should be done. Based on your progress, he/she can increase the level of difficulty to gradually challenge your brain.

Brain Exercises (Main Session)

 1 Look carefully at the following pairs of images and try to spot differences.

9 differences

2 Try to find all hidden items in the picture and circle them.

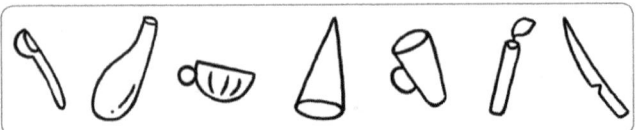

3 On this page are numbers. Without lifting your pencil from the paper draw a line between the multiples of 3 respectively as fast as you can. Note that your drawn line should only pass one time from each number.

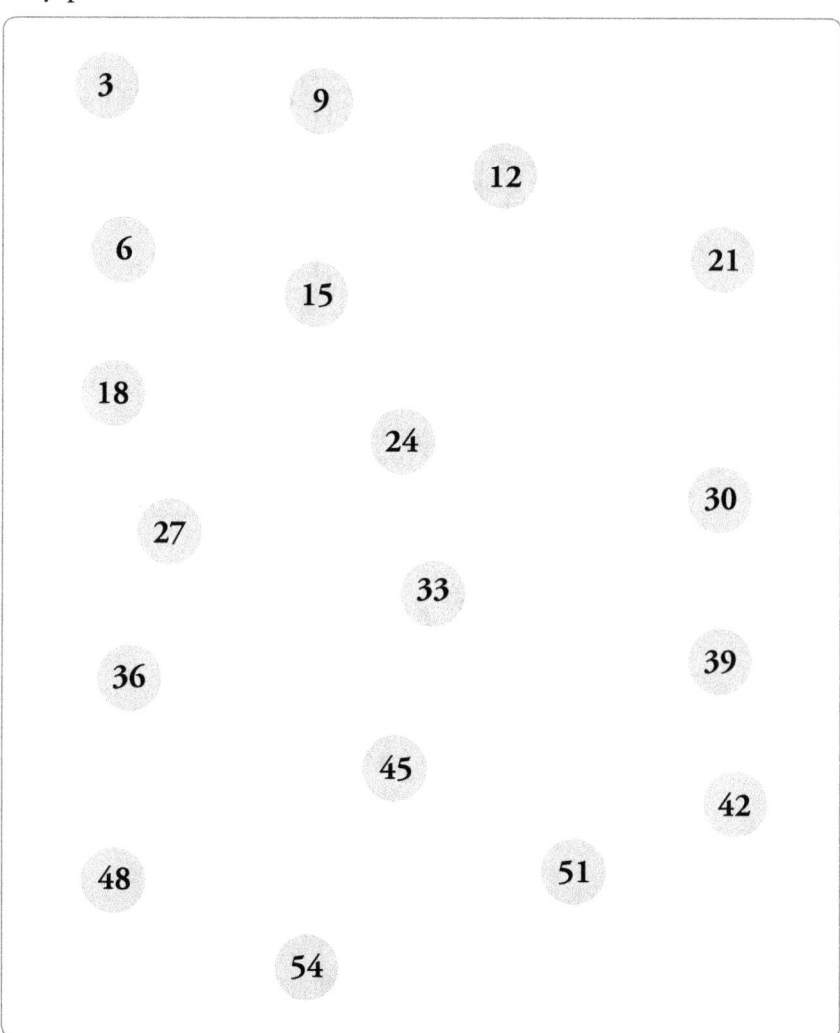

Time (sec):

4 Try to find a path between the gray and pink arrows that joins the entrance and the exit of the path.

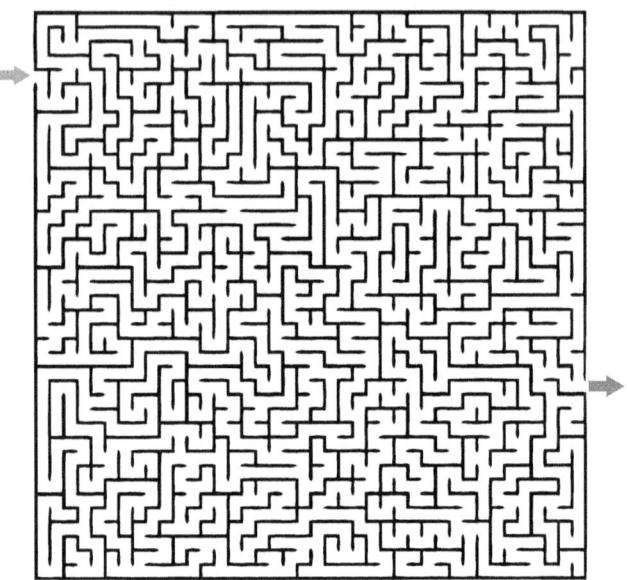

 5 How many squares and triangles are in this picture?

Number of squares:
Number of triangles:

6 See the below figure; then determine which figures below do not belong to the figure.

1

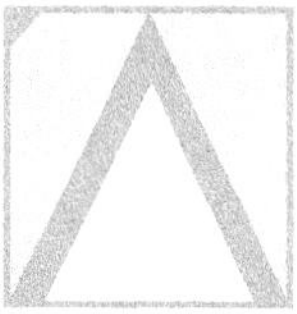
2

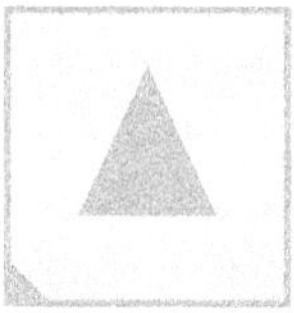
3

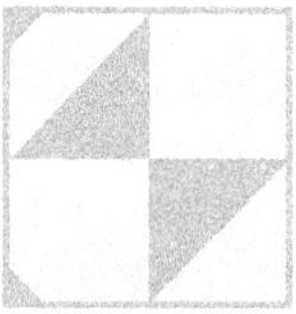
4

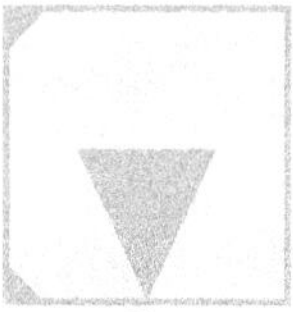
5

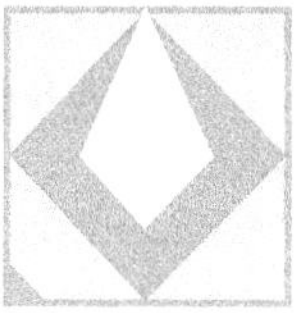
6

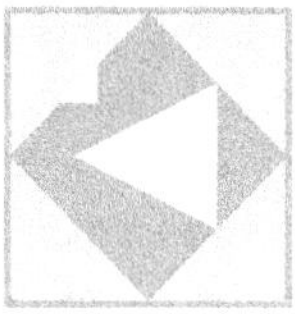
7

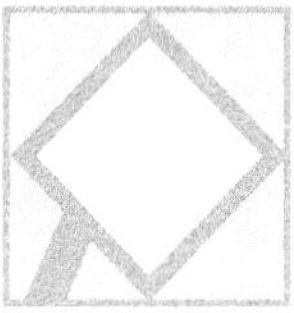
8

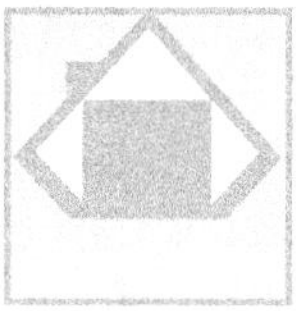
9

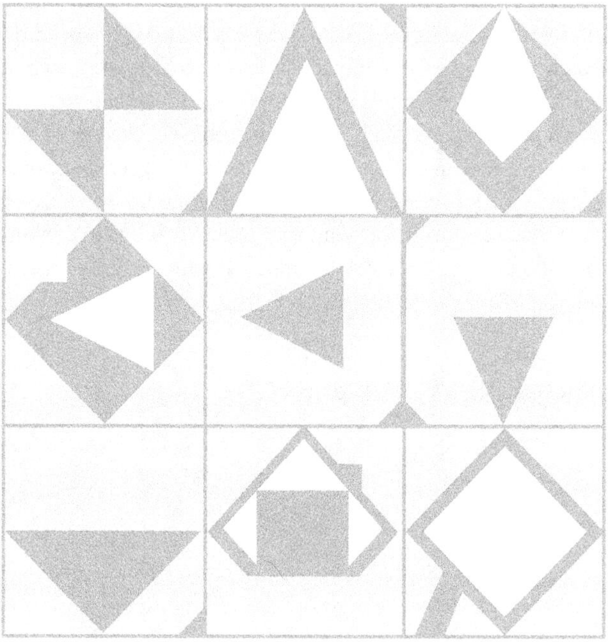

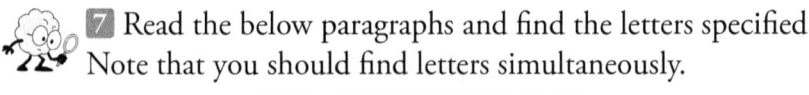

7 Read the below paragraphs and find the letters specified. Note that you should find letters simultaneously.

Letters "H/h","F/f","P/p","B/b"

The health benefits of spinach include improved eyesight, healthy blood pressure, stronger muscles, the prevention of age-related macular degeneration, cataracts, atherosclerosis, heart attacks, neurological benefits, bone mineralization, anti-ulcerative and anti-cancerous benefits, skin protection, healthy fetal development, and boosted growth for infants. Spinach is a green, leafy vegetable that is cheap and affordable for everyone. It is a rich source of minerals, vitamins, pigments and phytonutrients. All of these together make spinach very beneficial for a number of vital processes. Due to the vast range of benefits from this vegetable, it is advisable to consume spinach on a regular basis. Spinach is a member of the Aramanthaceae family and its scientific name is Spinacia oleracea. One of the biggest reasons why spinach is so important and valued around the world is that it is very durable. It can even survive through the winter and be just as healthy in the spring. Spinach is native to the Middle East, and was cultivated in Persia thousands of years ago. From there, it was brought east into China, approximately 1,500 years ago. It made its way into Europe a few hundred years later and quickly became a staple in a number of cultural cuisines. It can be eaten raw as a part of many salads, and it can also be cooked or sauteed down into a reduced form. This can be eaten as a side dish vegetable, or included in a number of recipes for soups, stews, and casseroles. It has been used in various parts of the world as a medicinal plant specifically included in cooking to help increase overall health. Let's take a closer look at why this leafy vegetable is such an integral part of our overall health.

Number of letters "H/h","F/f","P/p","B/b":

8 Look at the below image and try to find a pair of gloves.

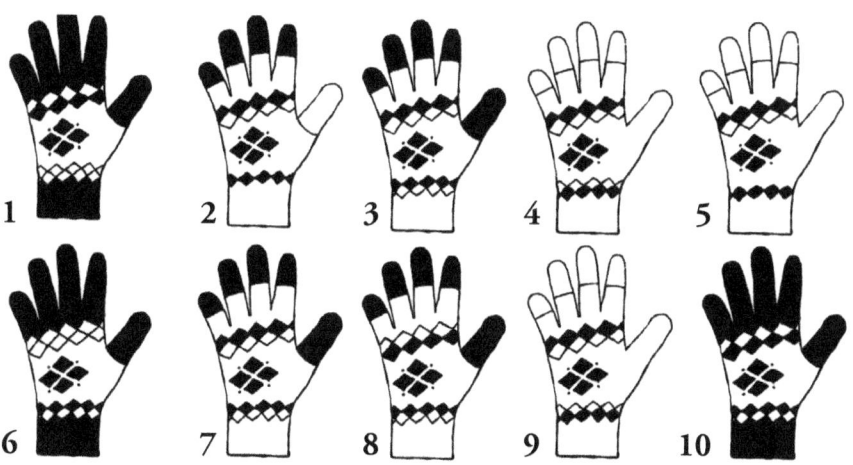

 9 Read the below paragraphs and try to count the word and also mark the fifth word each time simultaneously.

Winter is the coldest season of the year in polar and temperate climates, between autumn and spring. Winter is caused by the axis of the Earth in that hemisphere being oriented away from the Sun. Different cultures define different dates as the start of winter, and some use a definition based on weather. When it is winter in the Northern Hemisphere, it is summer in the Southern Hemisphere, and vice versa. In many regions, winter is associated with snow and freezing temperatures. The moment of winter solstice is when the sun's elevation with respect to the North or South Pole is at its most negative value, meaning this day will have the shortest day and the longest night. The earliest sunset and latest sunrise dates outside the Polar Regions differ from the date of the winter solstice, however, and these depend on latitude, due to the variation in the solar day throughout the year caused by the Earth's elliptical orbit.

Number of words:

10 Look at the below image and try to redraw it after two times of rotation in direction shown below.

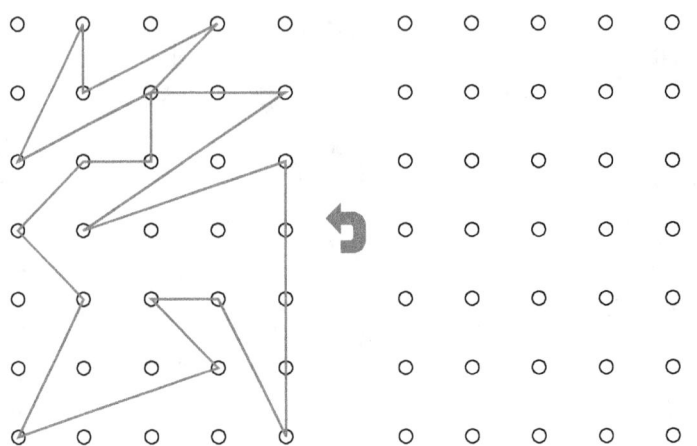

 11 Draw the other half of the picture.

Date   Number of incorrect answers   Time duration
Main weak points

Conclusion

Extra Exercises (Home-work)

 1 Look carefully at the following pairs of images and try to spot differences.

10 differences

2 Look at the faces below and try to identify emotion conveyed in each face.

① ② ③

④ ⑤

3 Read the below paragraphs and try to count the words and also mark the seventh word each time simultaneously.

> Sunflowers are usually tall annual or perennial plants that grow to a height of 300 centimetres or more. They bear one or more wide, terminal capitula (flower heads), with bright yellow ray florets at the outside and yellow or maroon, also known as a brown/red disc florets inside. Several ornamental cultivars of Helianthus annuus have red-colored ray florets; all of them stem from a single original mutant. During growth, sunflowers tilt during the day to face the sun, but stop once they begin blooming. This tracking of the sun in young sunflower heads is called heliotropism. By the time they are mature, sunflowers generally face east. The rough and hairy stem is branched in the upper part in wild plants but is usually unbranched in domesticated cultivars. The petiolate leaves are dentate and often sticky. The lower leaves are opposite, ovate or often heart-shaped.

Number of words:

4 See the below figure; then determine which figure below does not belong to the figure.

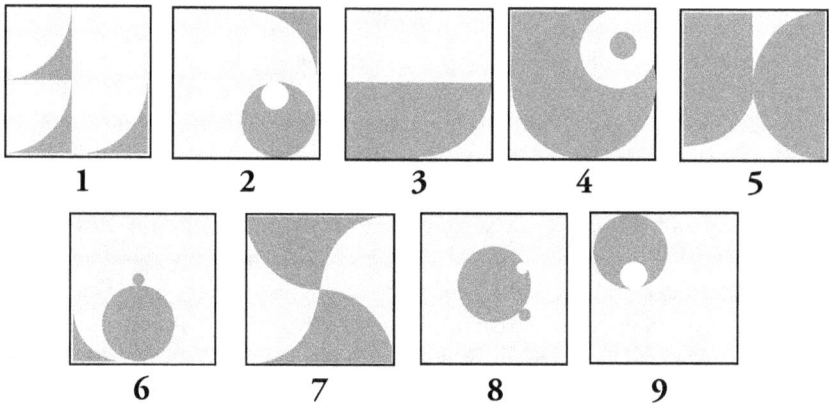

13th step | 213

5 Read the below paragraphs and find the letters specified. Note that you should find letters simultaneously.

Letters "D/d", "F/f"

Dog intelligence is the ability of the dog to perceive information and retain it as knowledge for applying to solve problems. Dogs have been shown to learn by inference. A study with Rico showed that he knew the labels of over 200 different items. He inferred the names of novel items by exclusion learning and correctly retrieved those novel items immediately and also 4 weeks after the initial exposure. Dogs have advanced memory skills. A study documented the learning and memory capabilities of a border collie, "Chaser", who had learned the names and could associate by verbal command over 1,000 words. Dogs are able to read and react appropriately to human body language such as gesturing and pointing, and to understand human voice commands. Dogs demonstrate a theory of mind by engaging in deception. An experimental study showed compelling evidence that Australian dingos can outperform domestic dogs in non-social problem-solving, indicating that domestic dogs may have lost much of their original problem-solving abilities once they joined humans. Another study indicated that after undergoing training to solve a simple manipulation task, dogs that are faced with an insoluble version of the same problem look at the human, while socialized wolves do not. Modern domestic dogs use humans to solve their problems for them. Dog communication is about how dogs "speak" to each other, how they understand messages that humans send to them, and how humans can translate the ideas that dogs are trying to transmit. These communication behaviors include eye gaze, facial expression, vocalization, body posture. Humans communicate with dogs by using vocalization, hand signals and body posture.

Number of letter "D/d","F/f":

6 How many fish are in this picture?

fishes

7 In this exercise, you can see different boxes including numbers with different repetitions. For the first part of exercise, read just the number but for the second part accurately identify the number of repetitions for each number. Record your time for both parts and compare them.

Part 1: Number

1 1 1	2	3 3	4 4	5 5 5
4	5 5	3	6 6	2 2 2
5	1 1	2 2 2 2	4 4 4	5 5 5 5

Time (sec): .... Number of errors: ....

Part 2: Number of repetitions

1 1 1	2	3 3	4 4	5 5 5
4	5 5	3	6 6	2 2 2
5	1 1	2 2 2 2	4 4 4	5 5 5 5

Report Card

Date   Number of incorrect answers   Time duration

Main weak points

Conclusion

Brain Club
14th Session

Brain Education

1 Which one is better: Computerized or Paper-pencil exercises?

Brain training exercise, either computerized or paper-pencil exercises have their own advantages. For example, in computerized exercises your speed or reaction time can be trained more precisely. But in a paper-pencil exercise, you can have closer interaction with your coach to offer you clear feed-back. For this reason, the combination of computerized and paper-pencil exercises could also be recommended.

2 Do you recommend any specific computerized or paper and pencil brain training program?

No! Depending on the level of your brain function impairments, your therapist/counsellor could recommend the most suited training program, suggesting either a computerized or paper and pencil program (or even the integration of both types). Most of these training tools include brain puzzles and games which are termed as "restorative exercises". In addition to these exercises, brain training programs may include a set of "compensatory strategies" taught by a therapist/counsellor to clients. The main purpose of these strategies is to help patients use external aids or techniques to compensate for his/her deficits. For example, using notebook or mnemonic strategies can help restore memory and reduce memory load to enhance the retention of information.

Brain Exercises (Main Session)

1 fill the gaps with words in the box. Each word should be used once.

Words: trigger- alleviate -diet -disorders- apples- age- dermatological

Acne is one of the most irritating skin _____ that can affect people of any _____ With a good amount of fruit in your _____, you can naturally curb this problem rather than opting for expensive _____ creams. Acne mostly occurs from skin infections and dermatological issues, but there are other reasons for such eruptions as well. _____ are the best option for treating acne; eat the skin of the apple, which has a high level of pectin that helps with constipation, which can be a _____ for acne. Bananas also helps to _____ acne, as it is high in fiber that again relieves constipation.

2 Try to solve the below Sudoku puzzle and note that each row, column, and nonet (sections of nine bordered cells) can contain each number (typically 1 to 9) exactly once.

			9		1			
			5	3	4			
3				4		8	5	6
	6		4				2	1
4			2	5	7			8
9	2				3		4	
7	1	6		2				9
		4		6	5			
		3			1			

3 Write the synonym.

a. Justice .... b. Avoidance ....

c. Reject .... d. Help ....

e. Reward .... f. Opinion ....

 4 Fill the empty cells with the correct numbers.

8	÷		×		=	6
+		-		-		-
	-	3	+	1	=	5
÷		+		+		×
3	×	2	-		=	
=		=		=		=
5	+		-		=	2

5 Look at the below pictures for 45 seconds and then turn to the next page and try to complete the image.

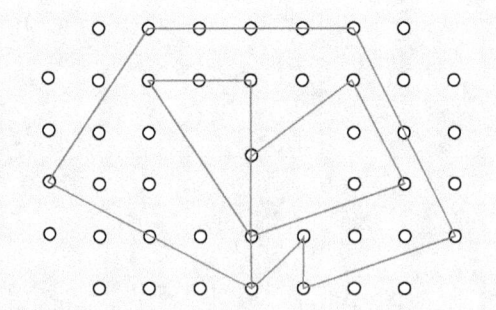

Try to complete the image below, without turning to previous page.

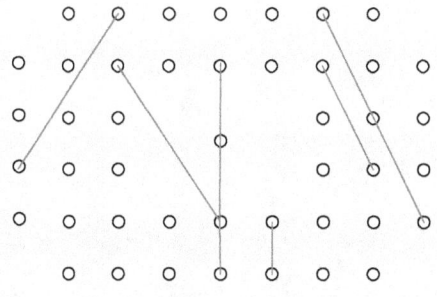

 6 Try to complete the cross-word.

Across

1. Gossip- 4. Current letters- 8. Large boat- 12. Egg on- 13. Gen Robert   - 14. Revere
16. Chair part- 17. Respiratory sound- 18. Away from each other- 19. Nosh- 20. Pull behind- 21. Depressed- 23. Born as- 24. Control direction- 26. Color your hair
28. See you later- 30. Pasture sound. 32. Enemies- 36. Very short pencil- 39. Pull along on the ground- 41.Correct- 42. Vase- 43. Striped Cat- 45. Before in verse
46. Fabricated- 48. Telltale sign- 49. Earth's satellite- 50. Small discoloration- 51. RR stop- 52. In the past- 54. "A" on cards- 56. Call off scrub- 60. Little devil- 63. Kind of doll- 65. Promos- 67. Director spike- 68. Pageant topper- 70. Be dependent- 72. In the know- 73. Stroke the strings- 74. Flatten wrinkles- 75. Baker's need- 76. Interim employee- 77. Tall woody plant- 78. Drenched

Down

1. Extraordinary- 2. Shooting marble- 3. Wager- 4. Aviation prefix- 5. Paw part
6. Penn neighbor- 7. Medicore grades- 8. Not to be trusted- 9. Move like a rabbit
10.   instant- 11. Sweat spot- 12. Utilises- 15. GPS reading- 20. Have a go at
22. Ruckus- 25. Diminish- 27. Small salamander- 29. N.Y. summer setting- 30. Molten rock- 31. Gothic arch- 33. Round cream filled cookie- 34. Foreign currency
35. Witnessed- 36. Additions- 37. Device for capturing- 38. Bring to ruin- 40. Chaotic mob- 44. Cellular material- 47. Airport acronym- 49. "GoodFellas" group- 51. Neptune's realm- 53. Petroleum- 55. Sore tight muscle- 57. Grayish green- 58. Start over- 59. Youth-
60. "   a Wonderful Life"- 61. Catcher's glove- 62. Trim- 64. Courage- 65. Lotion additive- 66. Physics unit- 69. Pirate's drink- 71. Make a mistake- 72. Said in surprise

[Crossword grid]

7 Look at the track below for 30 seconds and then go to the next page.

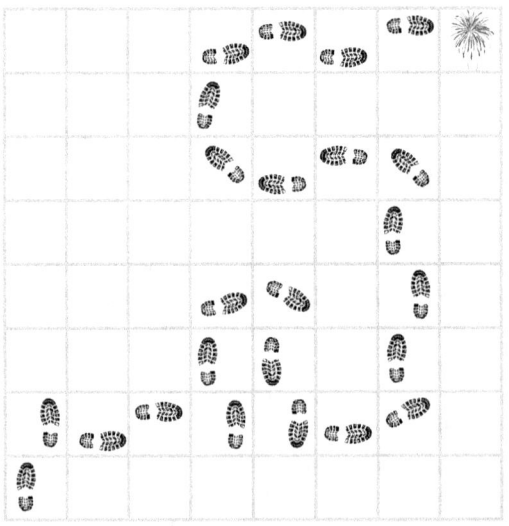

222 | Brain Club

Without turning to previous page, try to draw the track.

 8 What numbers should replace the question mark?

Part 1

1 2 / 6 × 3 = 3 ? / 8

   8   3   9   2   7
  a.   b.   c.   d.   e.

Part 2

5 2 5 × ? = 1 5 7 5

   9   7   6   5   3
  a.   b.   c.   d.   e.

9 Try to find the names of determined bedroom items in the below cross-word table.

L	R	R	T	A	L	A	R	M	C	L	O	C	K
D	D	D	O	E	S	R	S	H	E	E	T	S	S
D	R	W	P	R	S	P	A	S	T	C	R	E	H
N	T	E	E	T	R	O	B	D	A	P	L	R	E
A	M	E	S	O	S	I	L	T	I	O	R	O	L
T	S	K	D	S	U	S	M	C	E	O	D	S	F
S	N	P	S	D	I	S	R	E	P	P	I	L	S
T	I	R	T	D	Y	N	O	D	R	U	G	P	E
H	A	R	S	O	U	B	G	A	L	R	K	I	O
G	T	L	W	B	M	P	E	G	U	D	T	L	L
I	R	H	E	E	R	I	H	A	O	R	N	L	L
N	U	E	L	D	A	H	T	O	R	W	A	O	L
G	C	D	U	V	E	T	R	L	T	R	N	W	L
L	A	M	P	S	W	A	R	D	R	O	B	E	S

RADIO
DUVET
TEDDY BEAR
NIGHTSTAND
lAMP
DRESSING GOWN
PHOTO
CLOSET
RUG
PILLOW
ALARM CLOCK
SHELF
CURTAINS
BED
WARDROBE
SHEETS
MIRROR

Date   **Number of incorrect answers**   **Time duration**

Main weak points

Conclusion

Extra Exercises (Home-work)

1 fill the gaps with words in the box. Each word should be used once.

Words: resistance- factors- intake- weight -caffeine- aging- exercise- life

Blood pressure rises with ___ and the risk of becoming hypertensive in later ___ is considerable. Several environmental ___ influence blood pressure. High salt ___ raises the blood pressure in salt sensitive individuals; lack of ___, obesity, and depression can play a role in individual cases. The possible role of other factors such as ___ consumption, and vitamin D deficiency are less clear. Insulin ___, which is common in obesity and is a component of the metabolic syndrome, is also thought to contribute to hypertension. Events in early life, such as low birth ___, maternal smoking, and lack of breast feeding may be risk factors for adult essential hypertension.

2 Try to solve the below Sudoku puzzle and note that each row, column, and nonet (sections of nine bordered cells) can contain each number (typically 1 to 9) exactly once.

8	7			3			9	
4	3		6				7	
	1	2		7				
	9		3		6			
	2			6		8		
9			7			4	5	
5		3				6	2	

3 Write the antonyms.

a. Benefit .... b. Tidy ....

c. Brave .... d. Hinder ....

e. Plenty .... f. Victory ....

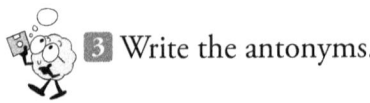 **4** Fill the empty cells with the correct numbers.

7	+		÷		=	3
-		-		×		+
	+	1	×	2	=	
×		+		÷		-
2	×		÷		=	
=		=		=		=
	-	6	×		=	6

 5 Look at the below pictures for 15 seconds and then turn to the next page.

Without returning to the previous page, try to redraw image you have seen in previous page.

 6 Try to complete the cross-word.

Across

1. Large body of water- 4. Facts and figures- 8. Pirate word- 12. Scheme to trick 13. Miner's quest- 14. Prove otherwise- 16. Strong affection- 17. Take ___ (doze) 18. Loses traction- 19. Sports facility- 21. Bone Prefix- 23. Clueless- 24. Affirmative 25. Pallid- 27. Co. leader- 29. Cattle group- 30. Bashful- 31. Mac alternatives- 34. Top of the line- 37. Burn soother- 38. Significant time period- 39. "... blackbirds baked in ___"- 40. Weep- 41. Microphone holder- 42. Human males- 43. Ray of light- 45. Charming for one- 47. Very wide shoe size- 48. Style of music- 49. Round cream filled cookie- 50. A dwarf- 51. Provoke- 52. Ruckus- 55. European capital- 59. Hawaiian dance- 61. Pizza topping- 63. Whooping bird- 65. Fill a suitcase- 67. Get a glimpse of 68. Athena's shield- 69.Just- 70. Trebek of TV- 71. Not firm- 72. Necessity 73. Crimson or ruby

Down

1. Composer's creation- 2. Gutter site- 3. Prayer ending- 4. ___ good deed- 5. Actor Schwarzenegger- 6. Torment: iritate- 7. Venomous snakes- 8. Abdominal muscles 9. Welcoming word- 10. Medley- 11. Kennel cries- 12. Murder- 15. Eastern Standard Time- 20. High point- 22. Repeat- 26. ___ you afraid of the dark?- 28. Organ of sight 29. Particular shade of a color- 30. Cunning- 31. Unskilled laborer- 32. Comfy summer shoe- 33. Identical- 34. British title- 35. Fencing weapon- 36. Court divider

37. Jacket part- 40. Salary Limit- 41. Book flap feature- 43. Brother (abbr.)- 44. Apiece 45. Professional- 46. Start over- 49. Soothsayer- 50. Jeans fabric- 51. Flying machine 52. Walkway- 53. Stupefied- 54. Shade of black- 55. Sony competitor- 56. City near Moscow- 57. Wise trio- 60. Straddling- 62. In the vicinity- 64. Psychic's claim 66. Elizabethan dramatist Thomas

7 Look at the below images for 15 seconds and then go to the next page.

Without turning to previous page try to draw the images.

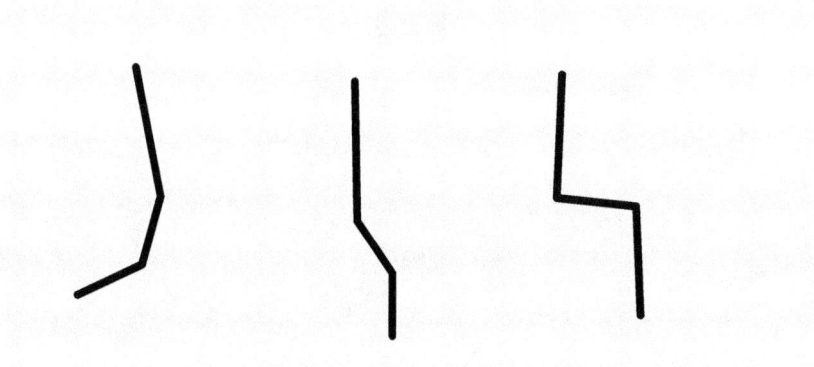

 8 Try to find a path between the gray and pink arrows that joins the entrance and the exit of the path.

 **9** What numbers should replace the question marks?

Part 1

1 2 0 × 2 / 5 = 3 ? 0

4	3	2	1	0
a.	b.	c.	d.	e.

Part 2

3 ? 9 - 1 8 3 = 1 7 6

7	6	5	4	3
a.	b.	c.	d.	e.

 10 What picture should replace the question marks?

Part 1

a.

b.

c.

d.

e.

Part 2

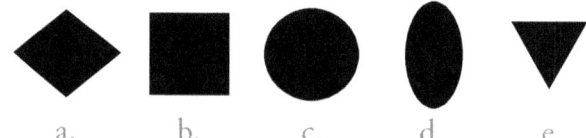

Part 3

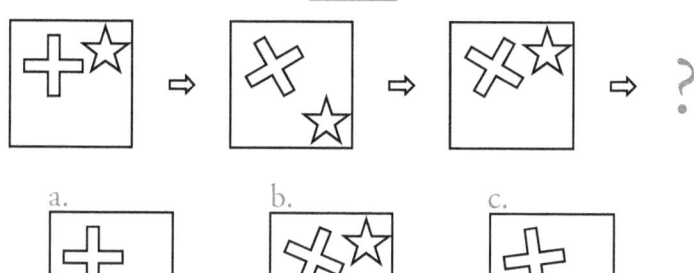

11. Look at the images and their associated numbers below for 15 seconds and then go for the next page.

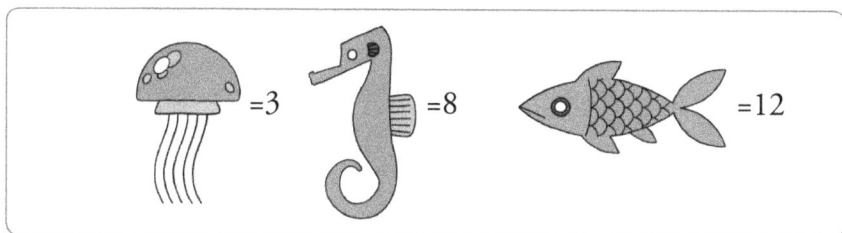

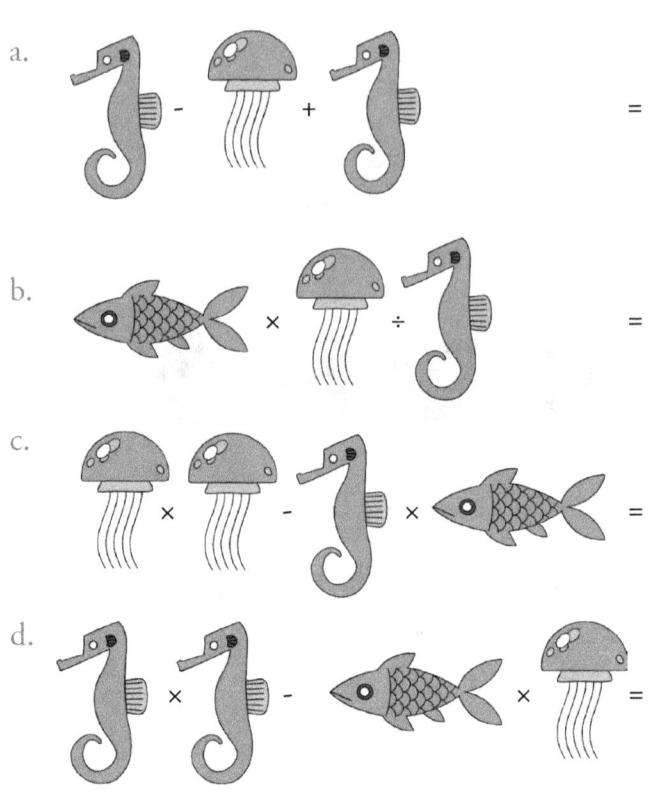

 **12** Draw the other half of the pictures.

Report Card

Date   Number of incorrect answers   Time duration

Main weak points

Conclusion

Brain Club
15th Session

# Brain Education

1 How long should I continue my brain exercises?

As we need physical exercises over a life time to stay fit and have strong muscles especially after damage has occurred, your brain needs brain exercise to achieve, maintain and increase its functions. You may need more specific and daily exercises at the early stages of training, but after a short time, you may need a routine program that boosts and then sustains your brain power. You can also adjust your exercises over time based on your daily application of brain functions in home, family, workplace, or other environments. For example, you can divide a 30-minutes daily training program into two 15-minutes parts, in the morning (before going to work) and during lunch time at work.

2 How can I become confident that my brain exercises will empower my brain functions in the daily life?

Your performance scores in certain exercises during a specific time span could help you to understand more about your progress in that specific exercise. But more important signs of your cognitive improvement are those which are present in your daily life activities through a process that we call the "transfer from games to life" effect. For example, recalling the name of the person whom you had recently met or acknowledging that you have been driving your car without an accident, might have been impossible for you before using brain training programs. But after practicing these exercises, you may be able see your significant improvement in these daily functions.

Brain Exercises (Main Session)

1 What number should replace the question mark to continue the sequence?

a. 3, 12, 48, 192, ?
b. 1, 1, 2, 3, 5, 8, ?
c. 2, 5, 10, 17, 26, ?
d. 5, 13, 29, 61, 125, ?

2 Write the synonym.

a. Admit

b. Brief

c. Persistent

d. Feeling

e. Excited

f. Valuable

3 Try to find a path between the gray and pink arrows that joins the entrance and the exit of the path.

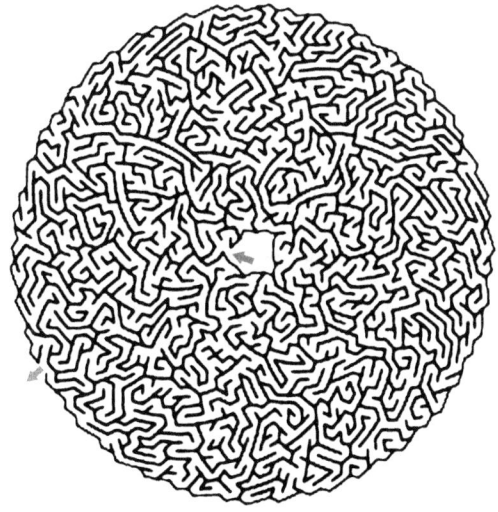

4 Try to solve the Sudoku puzzle below and note that each row, column, and nonet (sections of nine bordered cells) can contain each number (typically 1 to 9) exactly once.

						2		
1	7	3						
		4		7		8		
4		5	9					2
3			2	5				4
6					8	1		9
	1		6			3		
						9	4	1
		9						

 5 Try to describe the image below by writing a paragraph.

6 Look at the faces below and try to recognize emotion conveyed in each face.

 7 Try to find letters "p" and "q" simultaneously and circle them.

o	u	q	u	p	b	p	o	p
p	b	p	o	p	u	o	q	o
q	b	o	b	p	q	b	b	p
o	u	b	o	q	b	p	q	u
p	p	p	b	p	u	o	u	p
u	b	b	u	b	q	b	p	u
b	o	q	b	u	q	o	b	q
p	p	p	o	p	u	b	o	b
b	q	o	b	o	q	p	u	p

Number of letters "q" and "p":

8 Count the repetition of numbers "4" and "9" simultaneously and record it.

1, 1, 2, 2, 2, 2, 8, 7, 8, 8, 9, 5, 5, 6, 9, 6, 2, 6, 4, 5, 6, 4, 8
8, 1, 0, 1, 0, 1, 7, 9, 4, 0, 0, 2, 2, 5, 5, 6, 8, 9, 7, 7, 7, 3, 5
3, 5, 6, 5, 9, 8, 4, 5, 5, 1, 1, 4, 1, 2, 2, 6, 8, 3, 4, 3, 5, 6, 2
9, 6, 7, 8, 1, 7, 8, 5, 3, 8, 3, 4, 5, 7, 8, 8, 6, 9, 8, 8, 4

Number of "4":   **Number of "9":**

9 What picture should replace the question mark?

Part 1

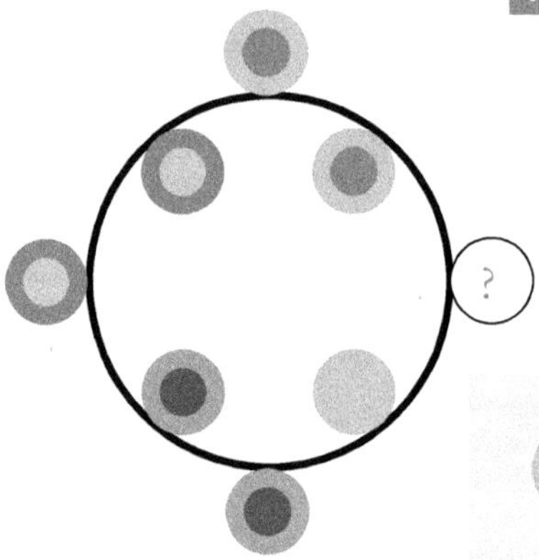

a.   b.   c.   d.

Part 2

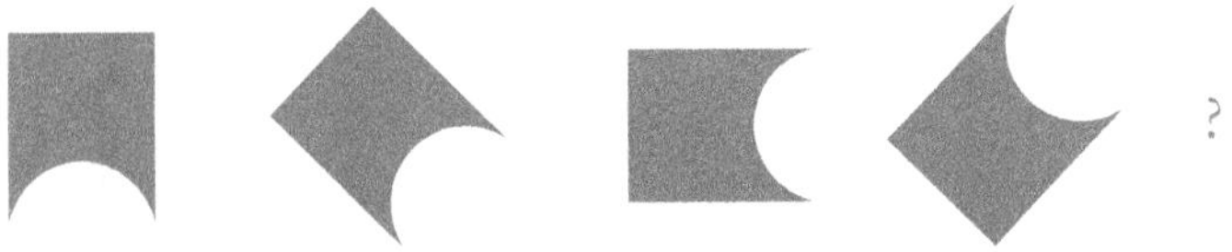

a.   b.   c.   d.

10 Write a paragraph with the name of images below and use each of them only once.

....

....

....

 11 If we put three images below together from the biggest to smallest one, what would be the result?

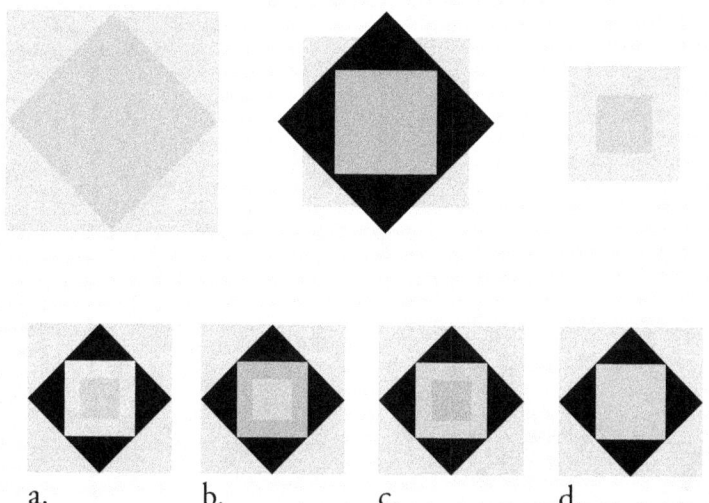

a.   b.   c.   d.

12 On this page are 20 cylinders. Without lifting your pencil from the paper, try to join all cylinders. Your drawn line should pass only one time through each cylinder and should not pass through circles. Try to do it as fast as you can.

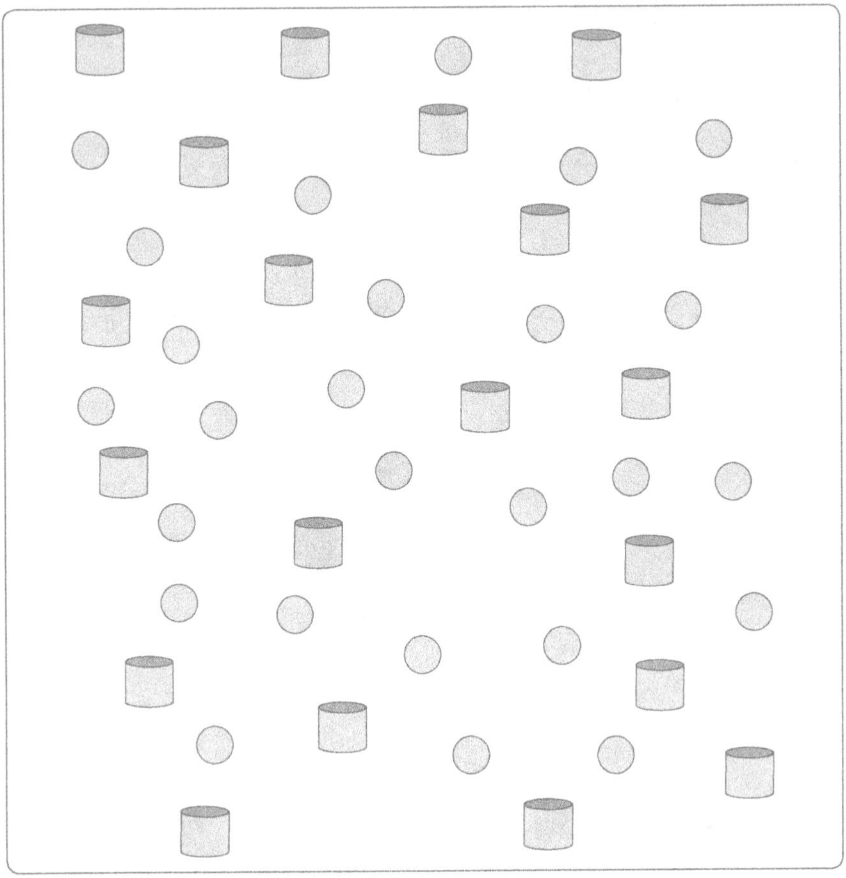

Time (sec): ....

13 Try to complete the cross-word.

Across

1. Linked computers acronym- 4. Greek salad ingredient- 8. Fourth dimension-12. Saintly ring- 13. Apple touchscreen- 14. Single- 16. Computer operator- 17. 2nd Greek letter- 18. Loses

traction- 19. Gun the engine- 20. Employ- 21. Talk too much- 23. Puncture sound- 24. Oaks and elms- 26. Alphabet sequence- 28. Inexperienced- 30. Picnic pest- 32. Coarse file- 36. Creative thought- 39. Proficient- 41. Holler- 42. Mesh fabric- 43. Phobia- 45. Pooh's young pal 46. Sharp taste- 48. Artistic- 49. Yeats or Keats, eg- 50. Uttered- 51. Dynamite- 52. Freudian subject- 54. Kimono sash- 56. Not together- 60. Propose- 63. Elect- 65. Navigational aid 67. Caviar- 68. Be in charge- 70. Mideast money- 72. Opens at an entrance- 73. Skirmish 74. Colored part of the eye- 75. Ms. Watson- 76. French holy women(abbr)- 77. Cuban coin 78. Used to be

Down

1. Surgical beam- 2. Tylenol alternative- 3. Neither's partner- 4. Lies- 5. Fencing weapon- 6. Tit for ___ - 7. "An apple ___ "- 8. Chores- 9. Of the same ___ (similar)- 10. Avril ou mai- 11. Brings to a halt- 12. Pain- 15. Double curved letter- 20. United States of America- 22. Sculpture or Painting- 25. Significant time period- 27. Sample- 29. Stack of money-30. Watchful- 31. Tidy 33. Prefix with dynamic- 34. Wild plum- 35. Scheme- 36. Division word- 37. Beloved 38. Sicilian volcano- 40. Fiber source- 44. Color your hair- 47. Mop & ___ (floor cleaner) 49. Soda drink- 51. Service gratuity- 53. Void- 55. Skeleton parts- 57. Fragrance- 58. Suite parts 59. Prefix meaning trillion- 60. Prepare for battle- 61. Observes- 62. Scot's skirt- 64. Expedition 65. But in France- 66. In addition to- 69. "Golly!" 71. Anger- 72. Morning moisture on grass

---

Date   **Number of incorrect answers**   **Time duration**

Main weak points

Conclusion

Report Card

Extra Exercises (Home-work)

 1 Calculate equations below and write the correct answer.

a. $24/250 \times 7 = ?$
b. $8 \times 6 \times 32 = ?$
c. $35/60 \times 3 + 20 \div 5 = ?$
d. $33/5 \times 6 \times 3 \div 5 = ?$
e. $9 \times 5 \times 35 = ?$

 2 Write the antonym.

a. Limited   b. Progress

c. Depressed   d. Active

e. Hidden   f. Hunter

 **3** Try to find a path between the gray and pink arrows that joins the entrance and the exit of the path.

4 What picture should replace the question mark?

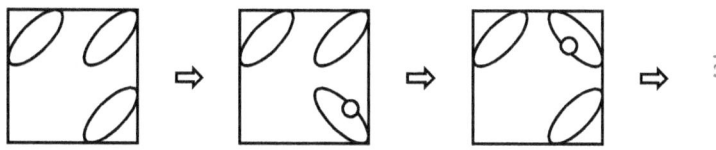

a. 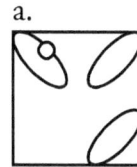 b. 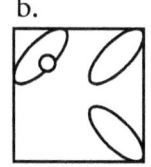 c.

5 Try to solve the Sudoku puzzle below and note that each row, column, and nonet (sections of nine bordered cells) can contain each number (typically 1 to 9) exactly once.

2								1
				1		4	7	
1			7		9		5	
3	4				1	2		
		7		2		6		
		6	5				1	3
	9		8		3			7
	8	2		6				
7								6

6 Look at the faces below and try to recognize emotion conveyed in each face.

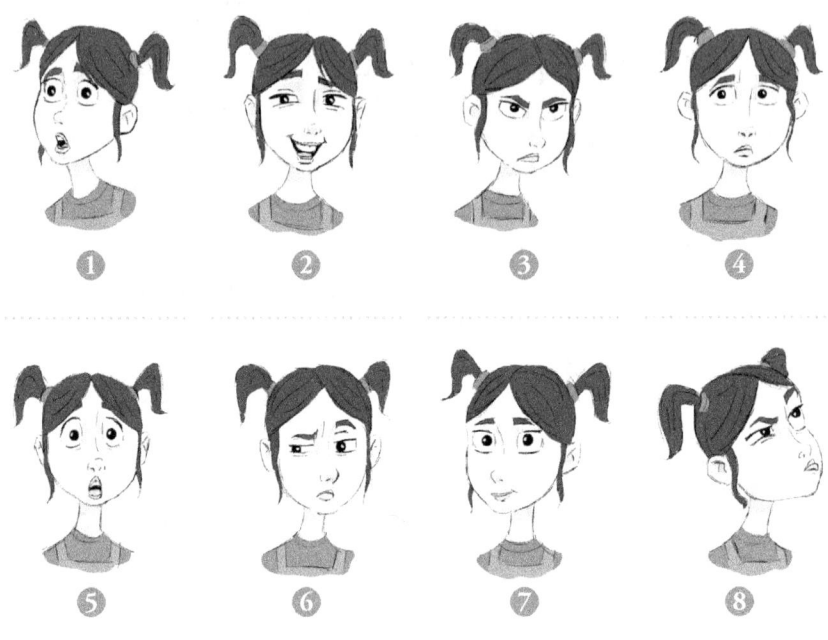

7 Count the repetition of numbers "3" and "7" simultaneously and record it.

1, 2, 3, 4, 4, 6, 7, 8, 8, 9, 9, 7, 4, 6, 7, 7, 6, 5, 7, 8, 6, 5, 6, 3, 5
3, 4, 8, 9, 9, 2, 1, 1, 7, 3, 3, 9, 5, 5, 7, 2, 2, 6, 6, 6, 9, 3, 8, 4

Number of "3":   **Number of "7":**

8 For each of the three pictures on the left, which of the images on the right would result from rotating the picture in the way shown by the arrow – 90 degrees counter-clockwise, 180 degrees and 90 degrees clockwise respectively?

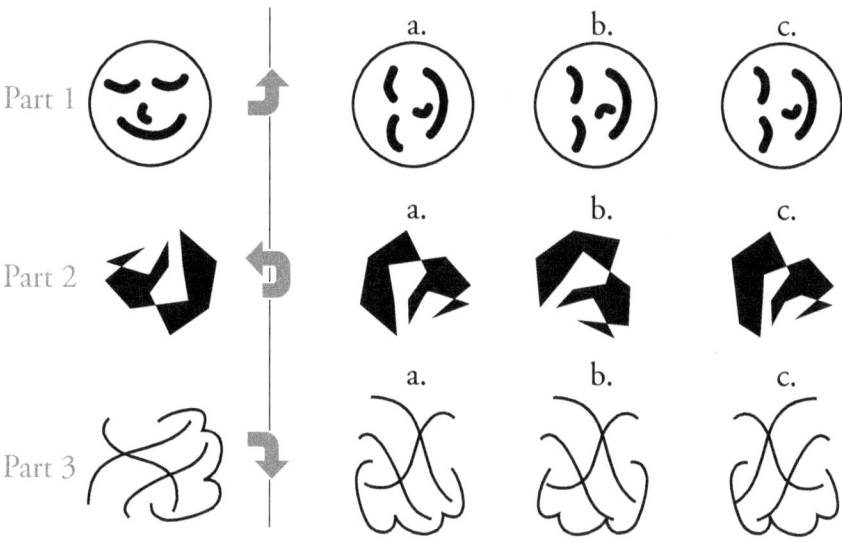

9 What picture should replace the question mark?

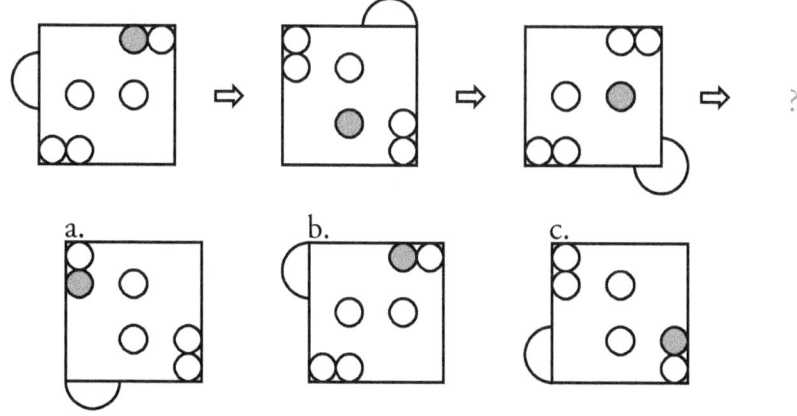

10 What picture should replace the question marks?

Part 1

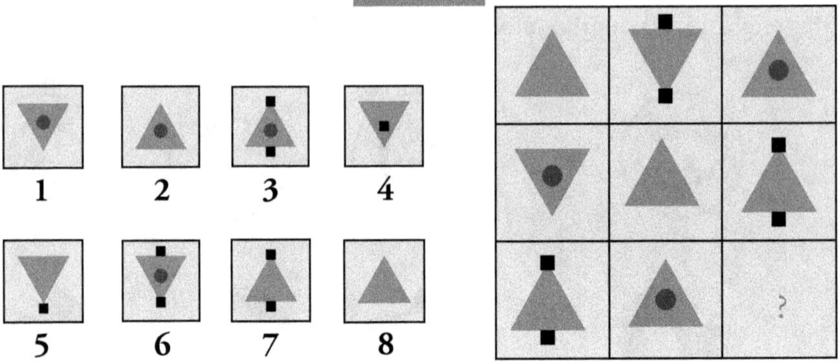

1 2 3 4
5 6 7 8

Part 2

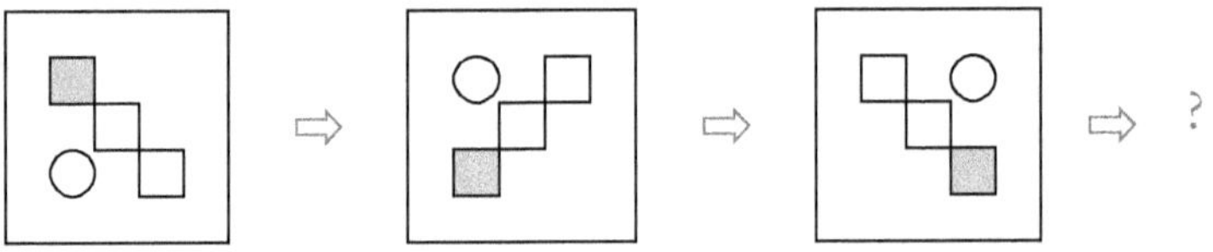

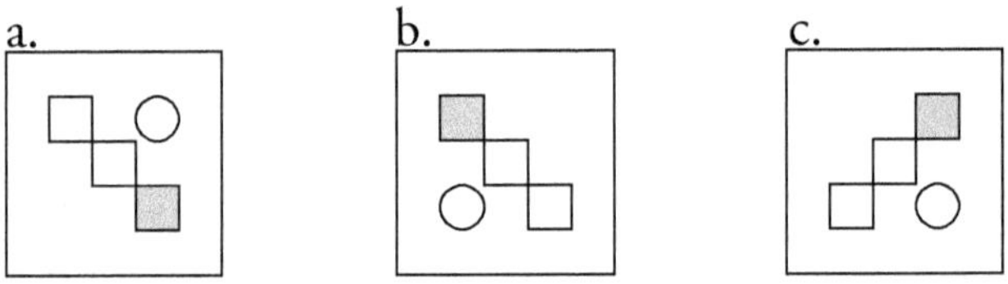

a.   b.   c.

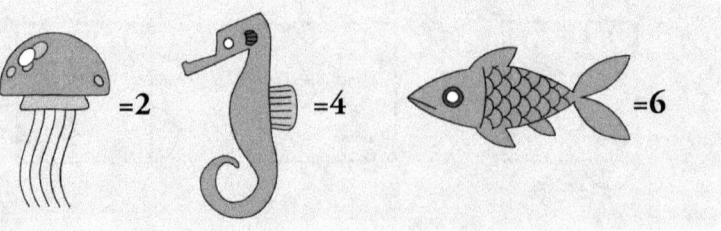 **11** Look at the images and their associated numbers below for 15 seconds and then go for the next page.

=2   =4   =6

246 | Brain Club

Without turning to previous page, try to calculate operations below.

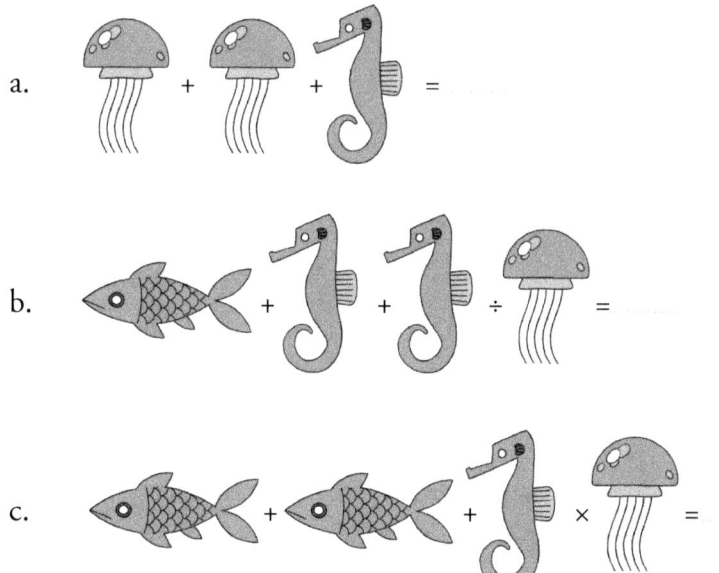

12 Look at the pictures below for 30 seconds and then turn to the next page and try to complete the image.

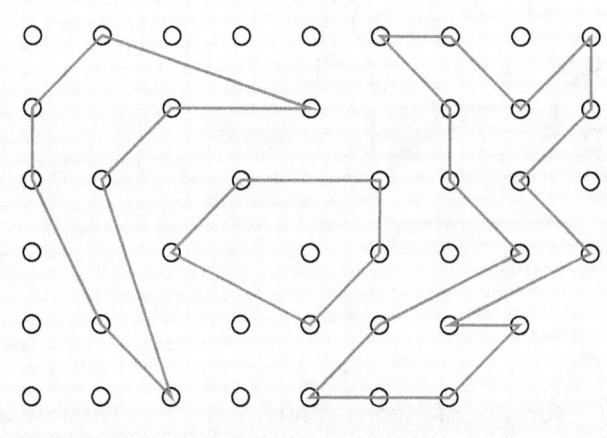

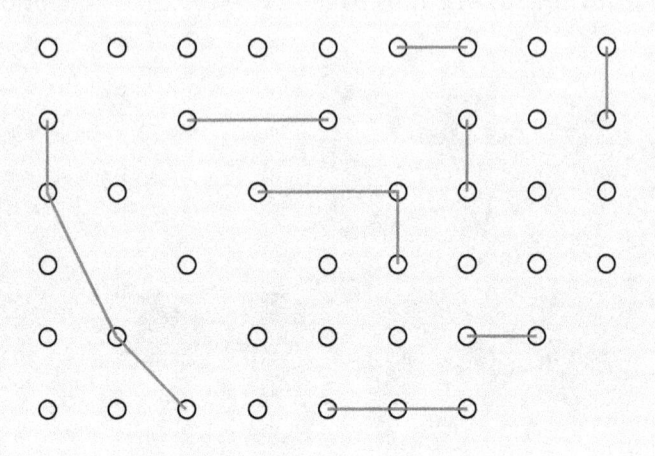

13 Copy the image shown on the left side as exactly as you can on the right side.

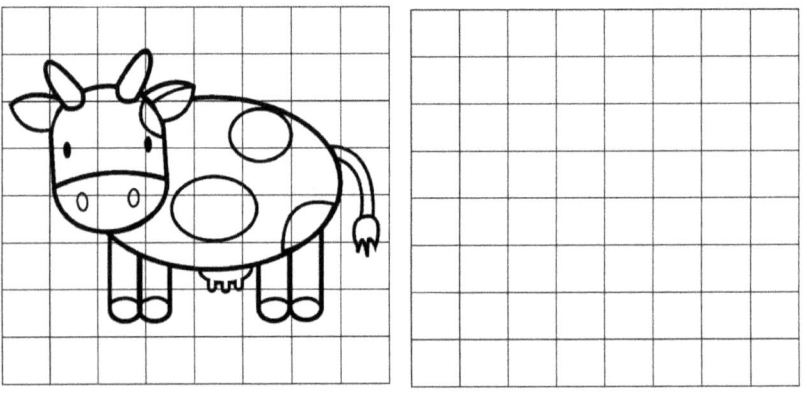

Report Card

Date   Number of incorrect answers   Time duration

Main weak points

Conclusion

Brain Club
16th Session

 Brain Education

1 A healthy brain is an absolute necessity for a happy, meaningful, and purposeful life. Chronic use of intoxicants such as: alcohol, cocaine, heroin, meth, OxyContin, marijuana and many others, regardless of whether they are legal or illegal can lead to serious brain impairment, even damage, dysfunction and greatly diminished brain functions. Fortunately, research shows that the human brain is capable of being restored or even improved in function in Recovery with the right approaches and exercises during abstinence. This restoration process takes time and intentional healing but achieving a high level of vitality in a brain once-damaged by addiction is very possible.

2 Your brain during early abstinence is like a broken hand. It needs your active support to be able to recover properly. After first weeks of abstinence, your brain will need active rehabilitation exercise to start to recover its own abilities over the time. The brain healing takes time but it is guaranteed if you pay enough time and attention to it.

3 Much like your body, your brain needs exercise on a regular and progressively more challenging basis. Our brain needs exercise to stay sharp and encourage resiliency to handle the day-to-day rigors of life. A healing, addicted brain needs even more attention, nurturing and care. In this educational book, we introduce some of the exercises which can be done easily, almost everywhere, anytime without any special equipment.

Brain Exercises (Main Session)

 1 Calculate equations below and write the correct answer.

a. $150 \times 9 = ?$
b. $103 - 2/68 = ?$
c. $9 \times 8 \times 2 = ?$
d. $(7 \times 2) + 20 = ?$
e. $30 \times 110 = ?$

 **2** Complete the following sayings.

a. You pays your money and you _____ .
b. Those who do not learn from _____ are _____ to repeat it.
c. The shoemaker's son always _____ .
d. The _____ is always greener on the other side of the _____ .

 3 Look at the below image and try to redraw it after determine rotation in direction shown below.

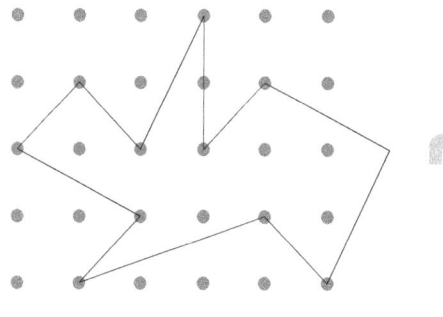

4 Read the paragraphs below and fine the letters specified for each part. Note that you should find letters simultaneously.

Letters "G/g","S/s"

Sensory memory holds sensory information less than one second after an item is perceived. The ability to look at an item and remember what it looked like with just a split second of observation, or memorization, is the example of sensory memory. It is out of cognitive control and is an automatic response. With very short presentations, participants often report that they seem to "see" more than they can actually report. The first experiments exploring this form of sensory memory were precisely conducted by George Sperling using the "partial report paradigm". Subjects were presented with a grid of 12 letters, arranged into three rows of four. After a brief presentation, subjects were then played either a high, medium or low tone, cuing them which of the rows to report. Based on these partial report experiments, Sperling was able to show that the capacity of sensory memory was approximately 12 items, but that it degraded very quickly (within a few hundred milliseconds). Because this form of memory degrades so quickly, participants would see the display but be unable to report all of the items (12 in the "whole report" procedure) before they decayed. This type of memory cannot be prolonged via rehearsal. Three types of sensory memories exist. Iconic memory is a fast decaying store of visual information; a type of sensory memory that briefly stores an image which has been perceived for a small duration. Echoic memory is a fast decaying store of auditory information, another type of sensory memory that briefly stores sounds that have been perceived for short durations. Haptic memory is a type of sensory memory that represents a database for touch stimuli.

Number of letters "G/g", "S/s":

 **5** Try to complete the cross-word below.

Across

1. Sunbathe- 4. Pie ___ mode- 7. Sugar serving- 11. Greek cheese- 12. Sir Guinness 13. Dried plum- 15. Part of the guts- 17. Pays to play- 18. Hawaiian garland- 19. " The Gift of the Magi" author- 21. Baking meas- 22. etcetera- 23. Dispute- 24. French heavenly being- 27. Fellow- 28. Fan sounds- 30. Bees live there- 33. In addition to 36. Treaties- 38. Related (to)- 39. Blunder- 40. Donald Duck nephew- 41. River's end 43. Chinese percussion instrument- 45. ipad software- 46. Greetings- 48. Outer edge 50. Certain Middle Easterner- 51. Guitarist Clapton- 53. Read only memory- 56. Carpet 58. Altercation- 60. French pal- 61. Pigtail- 64. Precedes in time- 66. Wading bird 67. Rests- 68. Lease- 69. Get a glimpse of- 70. Lock necessity- 71. Football stats

Down

1. Basic belief- 2. Top floor of a house- 3. Glasgow negative- 4. E.T or Alf- 5. 1974 Dustin Hoffman role- 6. Computer brand- 7. Book keeper (abbr)- 8. Ashes container 9. Shade of yellow- 10. Chemical suffixes- 11. Manicurist's tool- 12. Greek goddess 14. 6th sense- 16. Carbonated drink- 20. Slangy affirmative- 25. Wee drink- 26. Kind of cracker- 27. Coach- 28. Tattered- 29. Dance movement- 30. Owned- 31. Furniture chain- 32. Towns people- 34. Lower limbs- 35. Sellout sign- 37. ___ admin- 42. Cry of discovery- 44. Complains- 47. Tummy muscles- 49. Frosted- 51. Bert and Big Bird's friends- 52. Shabby- 53. Assessed- 54. Warning signs- 55. Atomizer spray- 56. Map abbr- 57. Strongly encourage- 59. Wine holder- 62. Back to school mo for many 63. Pen for pigs- 65. Sculpture or painting

6 How many cars are in this picture?

7 Look at the below image and try to remember the color and order of men for 15 seconds and then go to the next page.

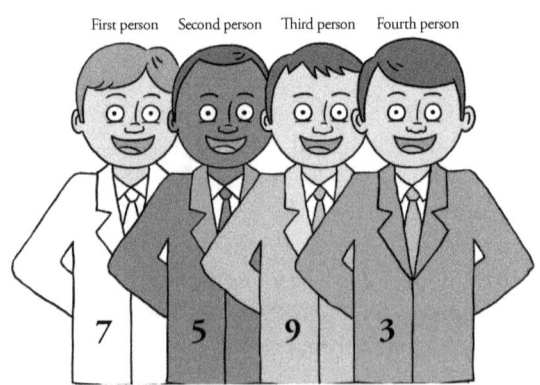

Without turning to previous page, try to answer these questions:
a. What was the sum of written numbers?

b. What was the number written on white shirt?

c. Where was the place of man with number 9 in the series?

 8 Look at the image below and details about players and scores.

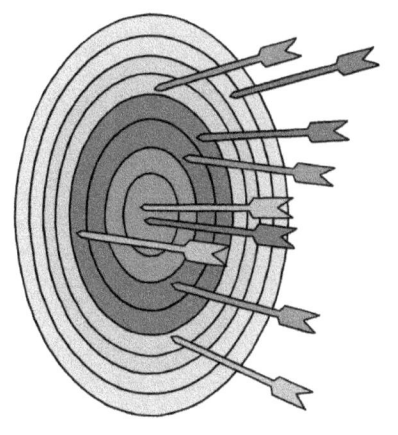

David
John
Simon

Score for each part

Interior pink section: 6   Interior red section: 10

Exterior pink section: 5   Exterior red section: 9

Interior gray section: 4   Interior black section: 8

Exterior gray section: 3   Exterior black section: 7

a. **Without turning to previous page, who was the winner?**

b. **What was the score achieved by Simon?**

c. **What was the sun score of David and John?**

 9 Find the odd one in this series.

a.

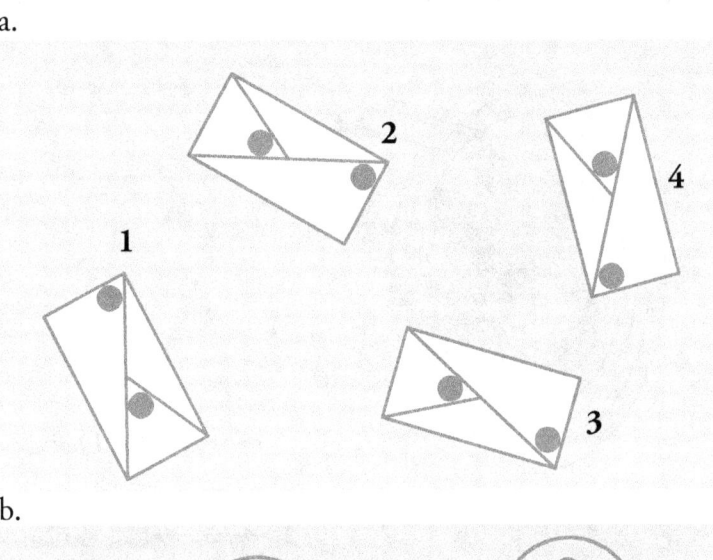

b.

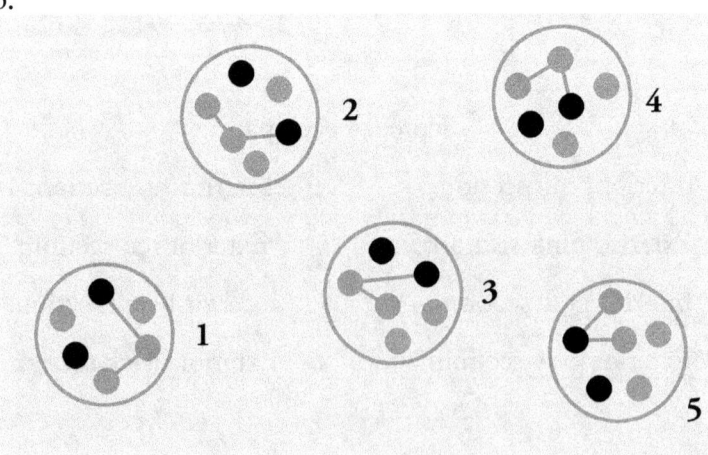

256 | Brain Club

 **10** What picture should replace the question mark?

The relation between these two images

is similar to this and image:

  1   2   3

  4   5   6

 11 Draw the other half of the picture.

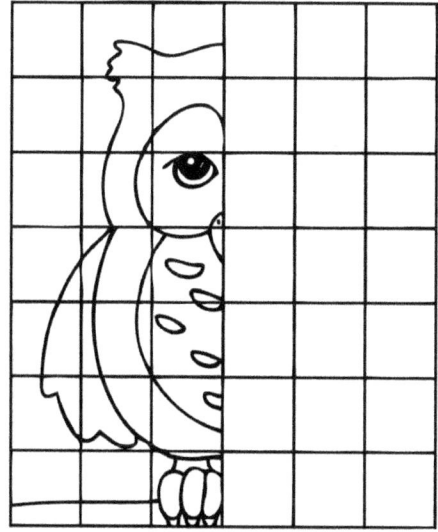

Date   **Number of incorrect answers**   **Time duration**
Main weak points

Conclusion

Extra Exercises (Home-work)

 1 Calculate equations below and write the correct answer.

a. 15/5 ÷ 5 = ?
b. 120 ÷ 4 ÷ 6 = ?
c. 60 - (36 ÷ (3 × 4)) = ?
d. (20 × 30) - 100 = ?
e. (20 × 25) + 60 = ?
f. (20 × 29) - 25 = ?

 **2** Complete the following sayings.

a. March comes in like a ...., and goes out like a ....
b. One .... of the world does not .... how the other half ....
c. Opportunity never .... at any man's ....

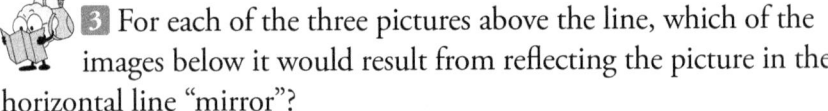 **3** For each of the three pictures above the line, which of the images below it would result from reflecting the picture in the horizontal line "mirror"?

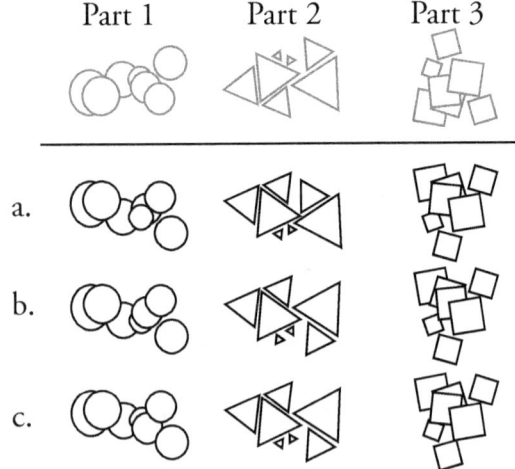

 **4** Try to complete the cross-word below.

1	2	3	4	5		6	7	8		9	10	11	12
13						14				15			
16						17				18			
19				20		21	22						
			23				24						
25	26	27		28		29			30		31	32	33	34
35			36		37			38		39				
40					41					42		43		
44				45		46						47		
48				49				50			51		52	
			53		54			55			56			
57	58	58	60				61					62	63	64
65						66	67			68			
69						70				71			
72						73				74			

Across

1. Kind of coffee and stew- 6. Perform a role- 9. Cash dispensers- 13. Gift recipient 14. Fib- 15. Hogwarts professor- 16. "Carmen" for me- 17. "Cheers" bartender 18. Attorney   - 19. Country surrounded by South Africa- 21. Big-billed bird- 23. First called- 24. Tiny particle- 25. Flatfoot- 28. Ho-hum- 30. Nary a soul- 35. Wait in hiding 37. Small amount- 39. "long time   "- 40. Oodles 2 wds- 41. Nasal cavity- 43. Ali and the 40 Thieves- 44. Big rigs- 46. Start of a recipe direction (2 wds)- 47. Biathlon gear 48. Subatomic particle- 50. Norway's capital- 52. Court fig- 53. Aquatic bird- 55.   la-la- 57. Time zone- 61. Peeper protector- 65. Scare- 66. Feeling down- 68. Must informally- 69. Staff again- 70. Scrambled or poached food- 71. NBC newsman Roger 72. Peggy and Spike- 73. Digit on foot- 74. Turnips in Scotland

Down

1.Something to worship- 2. Thick twine- 3. Chem suffixes- 4. Tree yielding boxwood 5. Warmed up- 6. Additionally- 7. Spy org- 8. Entice- 9. Against- 10. Soft mineral 11. Film-rating org- 12. Stitched up- 15. Food fish- 20. Elephant groups- 22. Indefinitely long time- 24. Desert- 25. Fastener- 26.   space- 27. TV teaser- 29. Melody for a single voice- 31. Bounces- 32. Japanese seaport- 33. Ledger entry- 34. Rising agent-36. Done with needles and yarn- 38. Some spa mixtures- 42. Like the sea- 45. Somber- 49. Neither here   there- 51. Washington neighbor- 54. Starting point- 56. Unaccompained- 57. Royal title below Marquis- 58. Away from the storm- 59. Not different- 60. Singing syllables- 61. Extreme side- 62. Suit to   - 63. Yugoslav town- 64. Dutch artist Frans- 67. Time gone by

5 In this exercise, you can see different boxes including one of four directions(left, right,up,down). For the first part of exercise, read just the direction but for the second part name the direction according to where they have been written in the box. Record time for both parts and compare them.

right	down	left	down
right	down	left	up
up	left	down	left
right	right	down	up

Time(sec): _____   **Number of errors:** _____

6 Look at the words below for 45 seconds and then turn to the next page.

sad- ready- eighteen- birthday-clock-school-happy-green- liar- yard-rainbow- bag- breakfast- file-student-red-road-tree

Without returning to the previous page, try to recall as many words as you can.

7 What picture should replace the question mark?

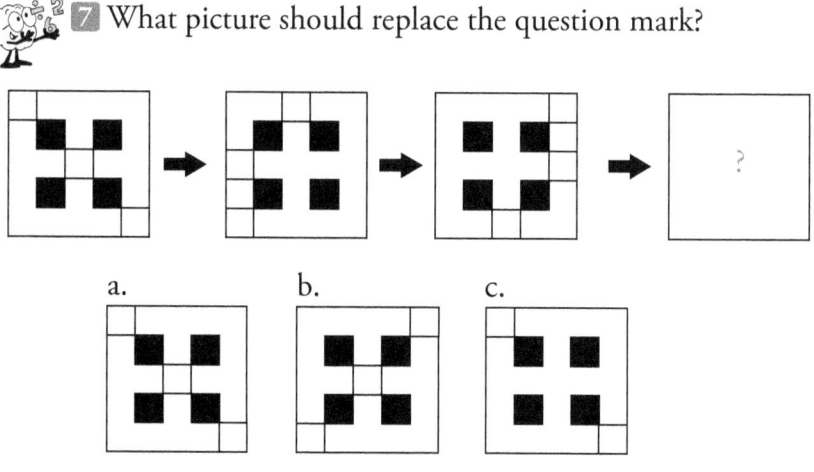

a. b. c.

8 Look at the pictures below for 15 seconds and then turn to the next page.

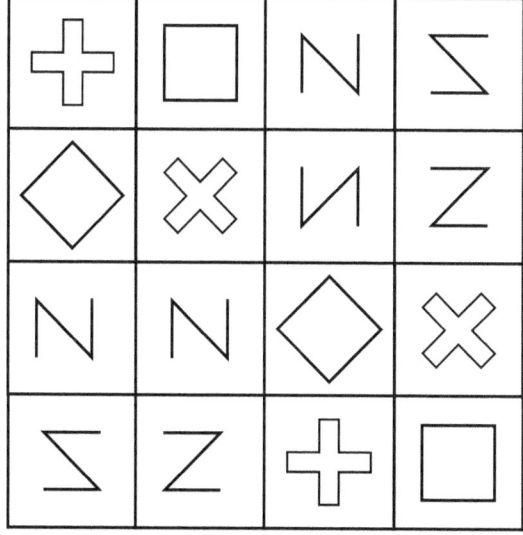

Without returning to the previous page, try to redraw image you have seen in previous page

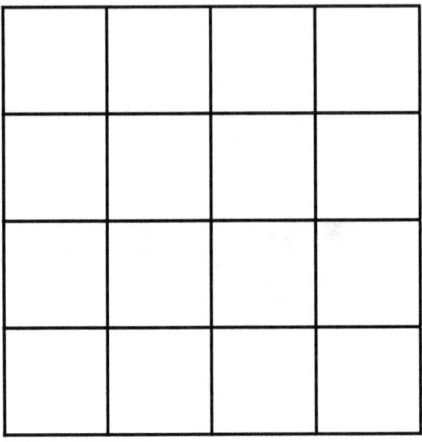

 9 Fill the empty cells with the correct mathematical symbol to arrive at the correct answer.

3		1		5	=	8
4		8		3	=	29
9		6		2	=	27
5		3		7	=	1
4		9			=	
=		=		=		
19		1		22		

10 Find the odd one in this series.

Part 1

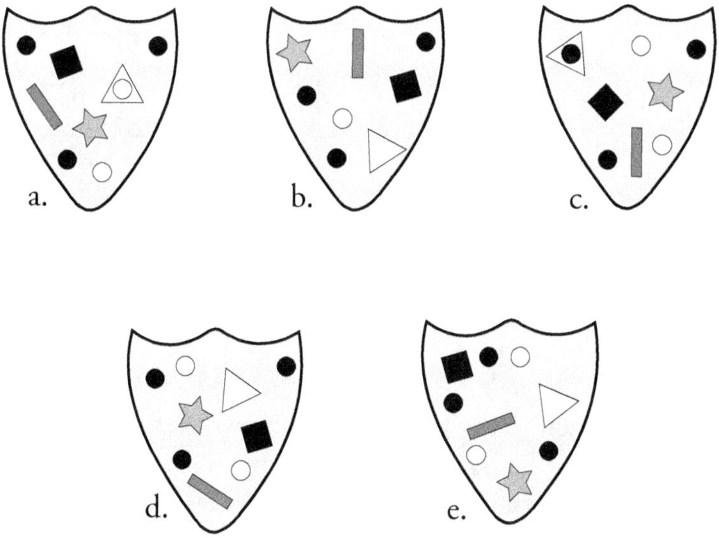

a. b. c.

d. e.

Part 2

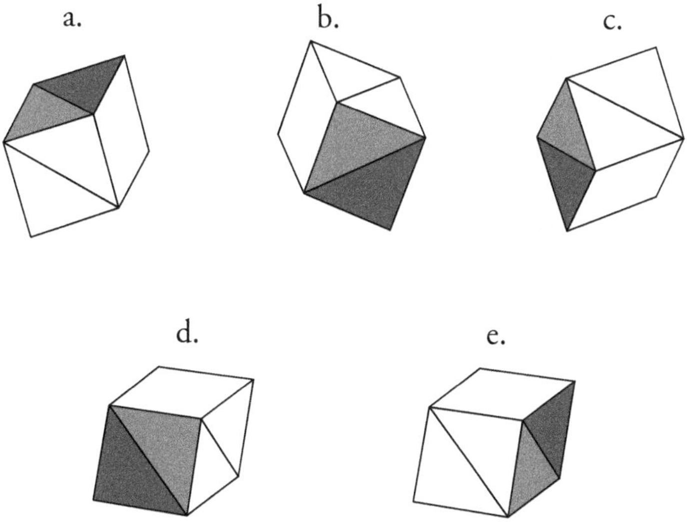

a. b. c.

d. e.

11 Draw the other half of the pictures.

  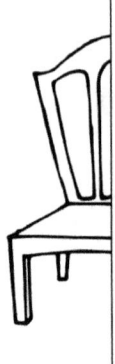

12 For each of the three pictures on the left, which of the images on the right would result from rotating the picture in the way shown by the arrow (90 degrees counter-clockwise, 180 degrees and 90 degrees clockwise respectively)?

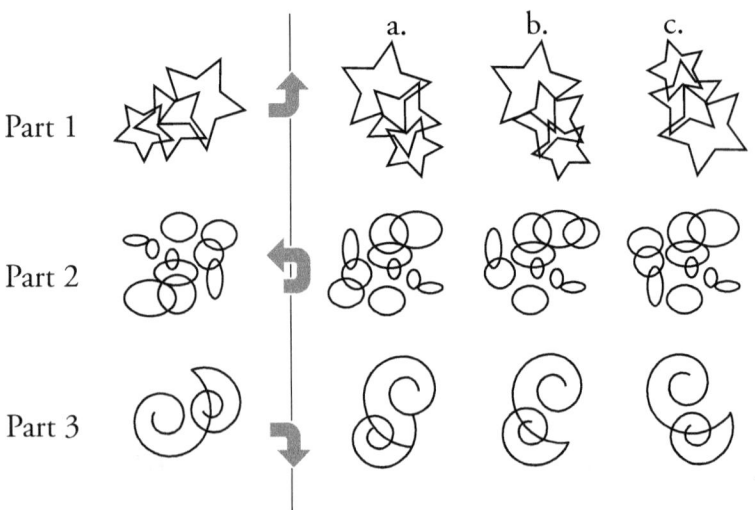

Date   **Number of incorrect answers**   **Time duration**

Main weak points

Conclusion

Answers

1st session
Brain Exercises

1

2

4 1. Surprise / 2. Anger
3. Suspicious
4. Disappointment

5

6

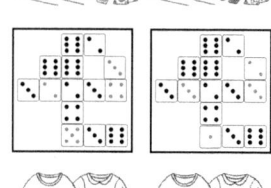

7 a. 60 / b. 25 / c. 21
d. 18 / e. 48 / f. 16 / g. 8
h. 24 / i. 11 / j. 20 / k. 5
l. 35 / m. 80 / n. 4 / o. 21
p. 28 / q. 40 / r. 55

8 a. 6 / b. 2 / c. 6 / d. 10
e. 3 / f. 11 / g. 72

9 a. 11 / b. 12 / c. 13 / d. 60
e. 64 / f. 99 / g. 60 / h. 42
i. 54

Extra Exercises

1

2

4 1. Joy / 2. Sadness
3. Confusion / 4. Surprise

5

6

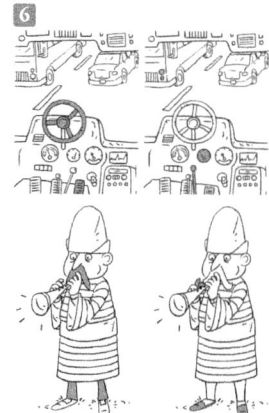

Answers | 265

7 a. 42 / b. 140 / c. 4
d. 26 / e. 8 / f. 125 / g. 43
h. 150 / i. 84 / j. 24 / k. 33
l. 28 / m. 15 / n. 11 / o. 63
p. 36

8 a. 10 / b. 3 / c. 9 / d. 9
e. 4 / f. 29 / g. 9

9 a. 18 / b. 48 / c. 36
d. 56 / e. 47 / f. 76 / g. 22
h. 24 / i. 42

2nd session
Brain Exercises

1 A.11 / B.16

3

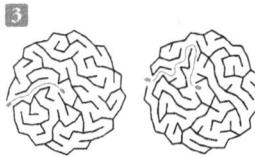

4 2,3,6

5

6 a

7

8 20

9 Number 3: 18
Number 8: 13

10 a. Right / b. Right
c. Left / d. Left

Extra Exercises

1 A.24 / A.24

3

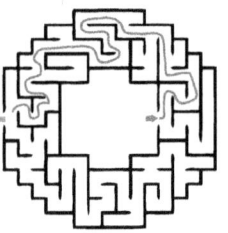

4 a

5 9

6 a. Right / b. Right
c. Right / d. Left

7 2,6

3rd session
Brain Exercises

2 d, c, d, c

3 b

4 3, 7

5 a. Truck / b. Apple
c. Camera

6 3, 6, 1, 2, 4, 5

7 d

9 Cellphone- Apple
Watch- Swatch / Jeans
Levi's / Sportswear- Nike
Burger- McDonalds
Coffee- Starbucks

11

4	3	6	1	7	8	2	5	9
5	7	8	2	9	6	1	4	3
9	2	1	3	4	5	6	7	8
6	9	3	4	8	1	7	2	5
7	1	2	5	6	9	3	8	4
8	4	5	7	2	3	9	1	6
1	8	9	6	5	7	4	3	2
2	6	7	8	3	4	5	9	1
3	5	4	9	1	2	8	6	7

13

R	A	W	A	Y	R	Y	A	Y	A	P	A	P	B
B	N	E	E	R	L	R	A	B	B	Y	E	E	L
N	A	E	B	R	M	R	N	E	A	R	W	A	U
B	N	S	A	E	P	E	R	N	N	R	A	I	E
R	A	A	P	B	E	B	E	P	E	E	T	B	B
S	B	L	B	K	E	P	O	E	A	B	E	N	E
E	S	I	R	C	A	S	A	P	T	W	R	K	R
E	Y	B	I	A	Y	A	E	E	E	A	M	L	R
G	E	R	W	L	O	R	E	P	N	R	E	Y	Y
N	P	R	I	B	B	N	M	L	T	T	L	M	M
A	A	A	K	C	O	R	E	R	L	S	O	O	N
R	R	A	R	M	A	E	L	I	M	E	N	E	C
O	G	S	E	G	N	M	P	E	B	R	K	I	T
S	P	L	A	E	E	L	P	P	A	B	E	W	I

Extra Exercises

2 c, b, a, a

3 a. 4,9 / b. 6

4 4,6

5 a. Flute / b. Oval
c. Cabinet

6 5, 3, 6, 2, 4, 1

8 a. 4,2 / b. ↑ →

9

4	8	7	3	5	1	9	6	2
9	1	5	4	2	6	7	8	3
2	3	6	7	8	9	5	4	1
3	9	4	8	1	5	6	2	7
1	6	2	9	7	4	3	5	8
5	7	8	2	6	3	1	9	4
6	4	3	1	9	8	2	7	5
7	5	1	6	4	2	8	3	9
8	2	9	5	3	7	4	1	6

10

¹G	R	²I	P		³W	⁴R	A	⁵P
A		M				U		A
⁶P	⁷O	P	⁸E		⁹S	E	¹⁰L	L
	R		¹¹S	I	T		E	
¹²I	D	E	S		¹³A	F	A	R
	E		¹⁴A	I	M		V	
¹⁵P	R	¹⁶A	Y		¹⁷P	¹⁸R	E	¹⁹Y
U		X				I		E
²⁰N	E	E	D		²¹S	P	O	T

12 A. b / B. a / C. a / D. c

4th session
Brain Exercises

1

2

4 Triangles with upward line:11, Triangles with downward line:10

5
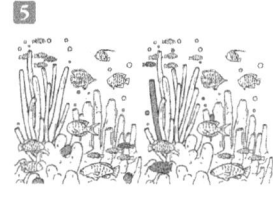

6 a. 77 / b. 50 / c. 26
d. 426 / e. 56 / f. 76
g. 68 / h. 80 / i. 76 / j. 63
k. 59 / l. 70 / m. 42 / n. 198

7 a. 25 × 2 / b. 3 / c. 69
d. 115 × 2 / e. 20 + 20
f. 44 × 2 / g. 46

8 a. 34 / b. 130
c. 12500000 / d. 216
e. 54 / f. 25 / g. 81 / h. 26

Extra Exercises

2

3

4 1. Joy / 2. Anticipation
3. Sadness / 4. Surprise

5 Squares with inner circle: 6, Circles with inner square: 7

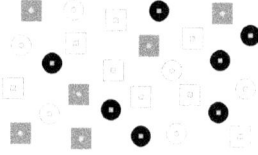

6

7 a. 32 / b. 28 / c. 3072
d. 567 / e. 20, 80 / f. 2484
g. 4, 3

8 a. 6 / b.1

9 a. 9,6,9,8 / b. 16,1,2.5,6

5th session
Brain Exercises

1 A. 23 / B. 41

3

4 M: 28 / N: 25

5 b

6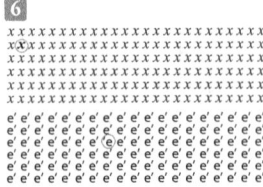

7 5, 6

8 Number of turning to left: 2, Number of turning to right: 3

9 Number of triangles: 24

Extra Exercises

1 A. 48 / B. 115

3 Number 4: 35
Number 7: 49

4

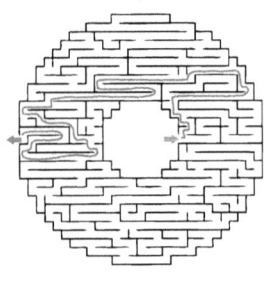

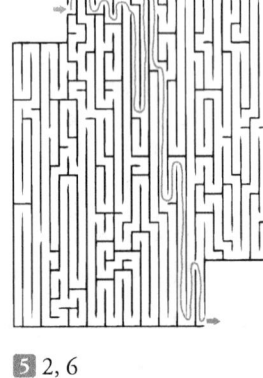

5 2, 6

6

7 3, 6, 8

8 Number of stars: 5
Number of triangles: 3

9 a. Right / b. Right
c. Left / d. Right

6th session
Brain Exercises

2 a. when in Rome, do as the Romans do / b. Hope for the best, but prepare for the worst. / c. Keep your friends close, and your enemies closer. / d. Never look a gift horse in the mouth. / e. you can't make an omelette without breaking a few eggs

3 Hamburger- Doorbell
Earthworm- Wallboard
Cupflower

4 a. ☿ / b. d / c. ♏

5 a. clock- hand
b. hand- job- candle
c. white- car

6 5

8
4 8 3 7 6 2 1 9 5
9 6 5 4 1 8 2 3 7
7 1 2 9 5 3 4 6 8
6 3 9 5 8 4 7 2 1
8 4 1 3 2 7 9 5 6
2 5 7 1 9 6 8 4 3
1 2 8 6 4 5 3 7 9
3 9 6 2 7 1 5 8 4
5 7 4 8 3 9 6 1 2

10 Part 1: c / Part 2: d

11 a. Rich / b. Ugly
c. Loser / d. Giving back
e. Disappear / f. awake

12 2 → b, 4 → c, 3 → b
4 → b

Extra Exercises

1 a. Don't bite the hand that feeds you / b. Beauty is in the eye of the beholder c. Necessity is the mother of invention/ d. you can't judge a book by its cover e. Good things come to those who wait

2 Sandwiches- Subway
Home accessories- IKEA
Camera- Canon
Car- Toyota
Chocolate- Toblerone

3 a. 5 / b. 2&6 / c. 3&4

4 a. Swimming- Boating
b. ski / c. Football- Basketball

5 Photo copy, ice cream, Hair brush, New born, High light, Six teen, Break fast, Out standing, sandwich, gold time

8
2 7 6 3 5 1 8 4 9
4 8 5 7 6 9 2 3 1
1 9 3 2 4 8 5 6 7
7 4 2 8 1 6 9 5 3
3 1 8 9 7 5 6 2 4
5 6 9 4 2 3 1 7 8
6 3 1 5 8 4 7 9 2
8 2 4 6 9 7 3 1 5
9 5 7 1 3 2 4 8 6

9 Part 1: a / Part 2: b

10 a. Clever / b. Sick
c. Cheap / d. Dirty / e. sunny
f. Unkindness

11 4 → b, 3 → b, 2 → c
3 → c, 4 → c

12
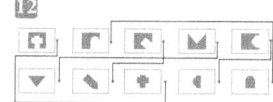

13 Number of turning to left: 3, Number of turning to right: 2

14
R	F	S	R	I	H	C	H	I	C	K	E	N	O
K	K	H	C	H	A	Y	G	T	O	N	P	K	B
H	T	E	O	M	A	K	A	G	O	O	S	E	B
A	U	E	P	E	C	E	A	L	O	L	H	B	B
H	R	P	I	K	T	A	O	G	B	H	N	I	F
O	K	N	G	A	A	N	G	G	P	F	S	H	G
A	E	A	E	B	A	S	E	E	R	O	E	P	I
H	Y	L	B	S	U	O	O	C	N	G	L	C	P
O	E	F	B	C	M	F	O	E	O	O	T	S	E
R	H	D	U	C	K	S	F	R	Y	S	T	W	M
S	M	L	L	A	M	A	C	A	F	P	A	O	H
E	L	A	M	B	E	P	S	S	L	E	C	C	G
E	O	P	N	U	C	L	U	T	Y	O	U	N	M
B	U	S	O	B	H	L	L	T	B	T	A	G	C

7th session
Brain Exercises

1

2

4 1. Anxious / 2. Surprise
3. Anger / 4. Sadness

5 ➡ = 12 / ⬅ = 9 / ⬆ = 9

6

7

8 a. 19 / b. 5 / c. 786
d. 430 / e. 570 / f. 560
g. 707 / h. 249 / i. 40
j. 577 / k. 642 / l. 3
m. 777 / n. 296

9

10 3

Extra Exercises

1

2

4 1. Anxious / 2. Anger
3. Fear / 4. Sadness

5 ▨ = 6 / ▨ = 8 / ▨ = 10

6 2 → c, 1 → c, 5 → b
1 → b, 4 → c, 3 → c
1 → a, 3 → a

7

8 c

9 a. 13 / b. 12

10 a. 46 / b. 46 / c. 19
d. 255 / e. 22, 27 / f. 532

8th session
Brain Exercises

1 Number of letters "G/g"
and "N/n": 15, 57
Number of letters "M/m"
and "P/p": 35, 17

3

4

5 1, 2, 9

6 Number of turning to
left: 5, Number of turning
to right: 3

7 20

8 17

Extra Exercises

1 Number of letters "B/b"
and "W/w": 40, 26

2 Number of letters "R/r"
and "U/u": 63, 45

4
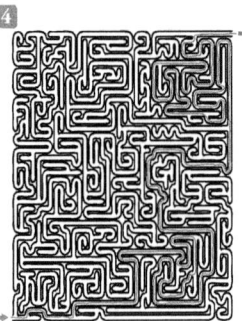

5 4

6

7 4, 5, 9

8 a

9 19

9th session
Brain Exercises

1 a. Finishing / b. Custom
c. Instructor / d. Visualization
e. Laugh / f. Forest

2 a. Loss / b. Repaired
c. Bright / d. Familiar
e. Cheerful / f. Seldom

3 c

4 2

5

H	A	T		A	S	T	I		S	H	O	O
S	E	M	I		R	O	A	D		H	E	I	S	T
O	R	A	L		E	A	S	E		A	R	L	E	S
L	B	S		E	A	R		A	P	R		S	S	E
E	S	S	A	Y				E	K	E				
			M	E	T		C	H	A		L	E	G	S
K	E	L	P		A	B	L	E		F	I	R	E	
E	T	A		B	R	A	W	L		R	A	E		
E	A	C	H		A	N	N	A		M	E	N	S	
P	L	E	A		I	N	K		B	I	O			
			D	O	C				I	M	A	G	E	
E	O	N		T	E	N		T	M	I		O	R	T
S	P	E	N	T		E	R	I	E		B	R	A	T
S	T	A	R	E		W	E	N	T		E	T	N	A
	S	T	A	R		S	T	Y	E		D	A	D	

7

1	3	4	6	7	8	9	5	2
9	8	6	3	2	5	4	1	7
2	7	5	9	1	4	3	6	8
4	2	9	1	5	3	7	8	6
8	1	3	7	9	6	5	2	4
5	6	7	4	8	2	1	9	3
6	9	1	8	3	7	2	4	5
7	5	8	2	4	9	6	3	1
3	4	2	5	6	1	8	7	9

8 5 → c, 3 → a, 5 → b
4 → a, 5 → a

9 Part 1: d / Part 2: a
Part 3: a

Extra Exercises

1 a. Aged / b. Smart
c. Ground / d. Conventional
e. Bonus / f. Hope

2 a. War / b. Cheerful
c. Privileged / d. Lie
e. Slow / f. Passive

3 A. b / B. b / C. a / D. c

4

T	S	K		S	W	A	T		A	N	T	I
T	I	M	E		A	E	R	O		L	O	O	P	Y
I	R	A	N		R	A	I	N		B	R	O	O	D
L	E	R		S	I	N		G	N	U		T	D	S
E	S	T	E	E				E	M	T				
			N	E	T		S	A	W		S	I	D	E
B	A	N	D		O	P	E	N		E	T	A	L	
I	R	E		P	O	I	N	T		C	D	S		
D	I	E	D		T	Z	A	R		T	H	E	E	
E	D	D	Y		U	S	E		Y	O	U			
			E	R	R				S	T	O	R	M	
B	O	W		O	N	E		S	S	E		C	E	E
I	D	A	H	O		W	E	E	N		S	T	E	M
B	O	R	E	S		O	R	E	O		P	E	S	O
	R	E	S	T		K	A	R	T		A	T	E	

5 7

6

9	8	1	6	3	2	7	5	4
3	6	4	7	8	5	1	2	9
2	5	7	4	1	9	3	8	6
7	1	2	8	5	6	9	4	3
4	9	6	1	2	3	8	7	5
8	3	5	9	4	7	2	6	1
1	2	3	5	6	8	4	9	7
6	4	9	2	7	1	5	3	8
5	7	8	3	9	4	6	1	2

7 5 → b, 2 → a, 5 → c
4 → c, 3 → a, 4 → a
5 → a

8 Part 1: a / Part 2: b
Part 3: c

9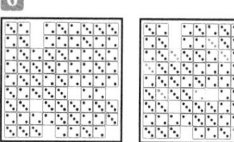

10th session
Brain Exercises

1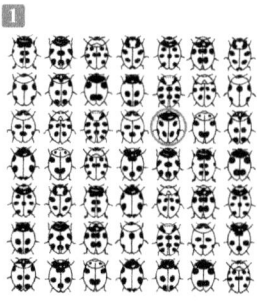

3 5

4 1. Anxious / 2. Surprise
3. Anger / 4. Joy
5. Fear

5 ♥: 5 / ♠: 9 / ♣: 7 / ♦: 10

6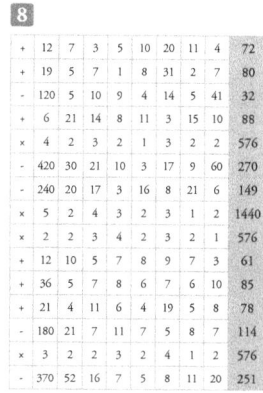

8

+	12	7	3	5	10	20	11	4	72
+	19	5	7	1	8	31	2	7	80
−	120	5	10	9	4	14	5	41	32
+	6	21	14	8	11	3	15	10	88
×	4	2	3	2	1	3	2	2	576
−	420	30	21	10	3	17	9	60	270
−	240	20	17	3	16	8	21	6	149
×	5	2	4	3	2	3	1	2	1440
×	2	2	3	4	2	3	2	1	576
+	12	10	5	7	8	9	7	3	61
+	36	5	7	8	6	7	6	10	85
×	21	4	11	6	4	19	5	8	78
−	180	21	7	11	7	5	8	7	114
×	3	2	2	3	2	4	1	2	576
−	370	52	16	7	5	8	11	20	251

9

1	×	3	+	5	=	8
+		×		+		
6	×	4	×	2	=	48
+		+		×		
7	+	8	+	9	=	24
=		=		=		
14		20		63		

9 a. (((3×5)+7)×2)-1
b. (((25×2)+5)×2)+7
c. (100×(7-1))+25-(2×3)
d. (((8+4)÷4)×75)+(6×5)

11 b

12

Extra Exercises

1

3 4

4 e

5 c

6 1. Fear/ 2. Anticipation
3. Anxious / 4. Angry
5. Sadness

7 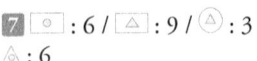 : 6 / △ : 9 / ⊚ : 3
△ : 6

8

9

3	×	7	-	5	=	16
×		×		×		
4	÷	1	×	2	=	8
×		+		+		
6	×	9	+	8	=	62
=		=		=		
72		16		18		

10 a. 127 / b. 315 / c. 52

11

12 b

13 9

11th session
Brain Exercises

1 T/t: 30 / Y/y: 33 / O/o: 20

3
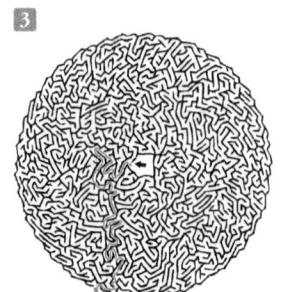

4
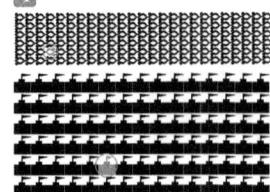

5 4, 6

6 2, 4, 6

7 a

8 Number of rectangles: 14
Number of triangles: 25

9 Figure 1: b / Figure 2: b
Figure 3: b

10 21

Extra Exercises

1 V/v: 11 / S/s: 115
H/h: 63

3

4 1, 7

5

6 Figure 1: cat- chocolate- mummy / Figure 2: candle bat- moon and cloud
Figure 3: hammer pumpkin- sweep / Figure 4: bone- spider- spider's web

7 a. Left / b. Right
c. Right / d. Right / e. Left
f. Right

8 18

9

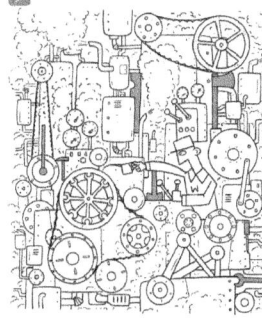

12th session
Brain Exercises

2 a. A golden key can open any door / b. A journey of a thousand miles begins with a single step / c. A person is known by the company he keep / d. After a storm comes calm / e. All good things must come to an end

4 a. candle- party- birthday girl- rain / b. find- playing children- park / c. opened window- beside- desk
d. yard- picture- family photographer

5 1, 4, 5

6 6, 8, 4, 7, 5, 3, 1, 2

7

1	6	3	5	4	9	7	2	8
4	8	2	3	1	7	5	6	9
9	7	5	6	8	2	1	4	3
2	5	7	9	3	4	8	1	6
8	9	4	1	7	6	3	5	2
6	3	1	2	5	8	9	7	4
7	1	9	4	2	3	6	8	5
5	4	6	8	9	1	2	3	7
3	2	8	7	6	5	4	9	1

9 3 → b / 5 → c / 4 → c
3 → c / 2 → b / 3 → b
4 → b / 5 → b

10

L E S		S L A M		S O A R
G A M E		N E R O		T A L O N
A S A P		A G E S		A R S O N
P S I		A G O	T A G	O D E
S O L A R			N E D	
	I T S		T U G	R Y E S
D O R M	A D E S			Y E L P
A B E		G R E E D		L I E
N O E L		U N D O		F L E D
E E L S		A B S	B Y E	
		D I D		E D G E S
E L I		M O M	P S S	R E M
M A N I A		O R A L		P E R U
S W I N G		R A C E		H A I G
S A N E		E Y E D		I T E

11 d

12 a

Extra Exercises

3 a. All roads lead to Rome
b. Ask a silly question and you get a silly answer
c. Behind every great man there's a woman / d. Don't cast your pearls before swine
e. Don't cross the bridge until you come to it

5 3, 7

6 a. disagreement- fans- football- discussion- radio
b. farms- damage- northern states- rain / c. present buying- store- window
d. picnic- friends- school morning

7

9	1	3	4	5	7	2	6	8
6	4	5	2	8	9	7	1	3
8	2	7	3	1	6	4	9	5
5	6	4	1	7	2	3	8	9
2	9	1	8	3	4	6	5	7
3	7	8	6	9	5	1	4	2
4	8	9	7	2	1	5	3	6
1	5	2	9	6	3	8	7	4
7	3	6	5	4	8	9	2	1

8

W A R		C A S A		S A S S	
S O B S		A L E S		C R A T E	
T R O T		L O C K		O F F E R	
O S U		O F T		S O W	E W E
A T T I C				A L S	
		A T E	O F F		U P O N
G R A N		S L U R		N E R O	
A I L		T E N E T		E C O	
B E A K		A C E S		B R A N	
E L S A		U S E		E M U	
		Y A K		O N I O N	
E B B		G E D	B O W		R H E
R A R E R		A C E D		A A A A	
G L A R E		W E E D		C T R L	
M E R E		N E T S		T E A	

9 Part 1: e / Part 2: 5

10 a. 22 / b. 16 / c. 7 / d. 8, 4

11 c

13th session
Brain Exercises

1

2

4

5 Square: 10 / Triangles: 21

6 4

7 H/h: 56, F/f: 35, P/p: 32 B/b: 26

8 1,10 / 3,7 / 4,9

9 160

Extra Exercises

1

2 1. Anger
2. Disappointment
3. Sadness / 4. Annoyance
5. Surprise

3 144

4 3

5 D/d: 71, F/f: 19

6 12

14th session
Brain Exercises

1 disorder- age- diet dermatological- Apples trigger- alleviate

2

6	4	5	9	7	8	1	3	2
1	8	2	5	3	6	4	9	7
3	7	9	1	4	2	8	5	6
5	6	7	4	8	9	3	2	1
4	3	1	2	5	7	9	6	8
9	2	8	6	1	3	7	4	5
7	1	6	3	2	4	5	8	9
8	9	4	7	6	5	2	1	3
2	5	3	8	9	1	6	7	4

3 a. Law / b. Prevention
c. Refuse / d. Aid / e. Bonus
f. Idea

4

8	÷	4	×	3	=	6
+		-		-		-
7	-	3	+	1	=	5
÷		+		+		×
3	×	2	-	4	=	2
=		=		=		=
5	+	3	-	6	=	2

6

S	E	A		D	A	T	A		A	H	O	Y
S	C	A	M		O	R	E	S		B	E	L	I	E
L	O	V	E		A	N	A	P		S	L	I	P	S
A	R	E	N	A		O	S	S	E		L	O	S	T
Y	E	S		P	A	L	E		C	E	O
				H	E	R	D		S	H	Y		P	C	S
D	E	L	U	X	E		A	L	O	E		E	R	A
A	P	I	E		C	R	Y		B	O	O	M
M	E	N		B	E	A	M		P	R	I	N	C	E
E	E	E		R	A	P		O	R	E	O
				D	O	C		P	R	O	D		A	D	O
R	O	M	E		H	U	L	A		O	N	I	O	N
C	R	A	N	E		P	A	C	K		E	S	P	Y
A	E	G	I	S		O	N	L	Y		A	L	E	X
L	I	M	P		N	E	E	D		R	E	D

8 Part 1: e / Part 2: e

9

L	R	R	T	A	L	A	R	M	C	L	O	C	K
D	D	D	O	E	S	R	S	H	E	E	T	S	S
D	R	W	P	R	S	P	A	S	T	C	R	E	H
N	T	E	E	T	R	O	B	D	A	P	L	R	E
A	M	E	S	O	S	I	L	T	I	O	R	O	L
T	S	K	D	S	U	S	M	C	E	O	D	S	F
S	N	P	S	D	I	S	R	E	P	P	I	L	S
T	I	R	T	D	Y	N	O	D	R	U	G	P	E
H	A	R	S	O	U	B	G	A	L	R	K	I	O
G	T	L	W	B	M	P	E	G	U	D	T	L	L
I	R	H	E	E	R	I	H	A	O	R	N	L	L
N	U	E	L	D	A	H	T	O	R	W	A	O	L
G	C	D	U	V	E	T	R	L	T	R	N	W	L
L	A	M	P	S	W	A	R	D	R	O	B	E	S

Extra Exercises

1 aging- life- factors- intake exercise- caffeine- resistance weight

274 | Brain Club

2

2	9	5	1	8	7	4	3	6
8	7	6	4	5	3	2	1	9
4	3	1	9	6	2	8	5	7
6	1	8	2	4	5	7	9	3
7	5	9	8	3	1	6	2	4
3	4	2	7	9	6	5	8	1
9	2	3	6	7	8	1	4	5
5	8	7	3	1	4	9	6	2
1	6	4	5	2	9	3	7	8

3 a. Loss / b. Dirty
c. Afraid / d. Aid / e. Lack
f. Failure

4

7	+	2	÷	3	=	3
-		-		×		+
3	+	1	×	2	=	8
×		+		÷		-
2	×	5	÷	2	=	5
=		=		=		=
8	-	6	×	3	=	6

6

G	A	B		A	C	D	C		S	H	I	P
U	R	G	E		E	L	E	E		H	O	N	O	R
S	E	A	T		R	A	L	E		A	P	A	R	T
E	A	T		T	O	W		S	A	D		N	E	E
S	T	E	E	R			D	Y	E					
			B	Y	E		M	O	O		F	O	E	S
S	T	U	B		D	R	A	G		T	R	U	E	
U	R	N		T	I	G	E	R		E	R	E		
M	A	D	E		O	M	E	N		M	O	O	N	
S	P	O	T		S	T	A		A	G	O			
		A	C	E				A	B	O	R	T		
I	M	P		R	A	G		A	D	S		L	E	E
T	I	A	R	A		R	E	L	Y		W	I	S	E
S	T	R	U	M		I	R	O	N		O	V	E	N
T	E	M	P		T	R	E	E		W	E	T		

8

9 Part 1: e / Part 2: c

10 Part 1: b / Part 2: b
Part 3: a

11 a. 13 / b. 4.5 / c. 12
d. 156

**15th session
Brain Exercises**

1 a. 768 / b. 13 / c. 37
d. 253

2 a. Accept / b. Small
c. Constant / d. Sense
e. Enthusiastic / f. Worthwhile

3

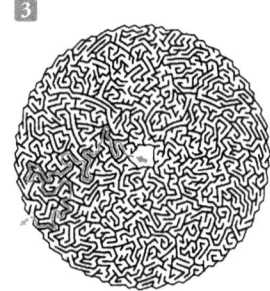

4

9	6	8	3	5	4	2	1	7
1	7	3	8	2	6	4	9	5
2	5	4	1	9	7	6	8	3
4	8	5	9	6	1	7	3	2
3	9	1	2	7	5	8	6	4
6	2	7	4	3	8	1	5	9
5	1	2	6	4	9	3	7	8
7	3	6	5	8	2	9	4	1
8	4	9	7	1	3	5	2	6

6 1. Aggressiveness
2. Worry / 3. Anticipation
4. Suspicious / 5. Joy
6. Sadness / 7. Thoughtful
8. Disappointment

7 Number of "q": 12
Number of "p": 21

8 Number 4: 8
Number 9: 7

9 Part 1: a / Part 2: a

11 a

13

L	A	N		F	E	T	A		T	I	M	E		
H	A	L	O		I	P	A	D		A	L	O	N	E
U	S	E	R		B	E	T	A		S	K	I	D	S
R	E	V		U	S	E		Y	A	K		S	S	S
T	R	E	E	S				R	S	T				
			R	A	W		A	N	T		R	A	S	P
I	D	E	A		A	B	L	E			Y	E	L	L
N	E	T		D	R	E	A	D			R	O	O	
T	A	N	G		A	R	T	Y		P	O	E	T	
O	R	A	L		T	N	T		E	G	O			
		O	B	I			A	P	A	R	T			
A	S	K		O	P	T		M	A	P		R	O	E
R	E	I	G	N		R	I	A	L		D	O	O	R
M	E	L	E	E		I	R	I	S		E	M	M	A
S	T	E	S		P	E	S	O		W	A	S		

Extra Exercises

1 a. 169/75 / b. 1536
c. 25/36 / d. 120/6 / e. 1575

2 a. Unrestricted
b. Decline / c. Happy
d. Lazy / e. Apparent / f. Prey

3

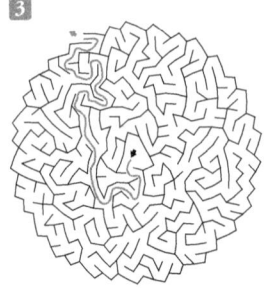

4 a

5

2	7	8	4	3	5	9	6	1
9	5	3	2	1	6	4	7	8
1	6	4	7	8	9	3	5	2
3	4	9	6	7	1	2	8	5
5	1	7	3	2	8	6	9	4
8	2	6	5	9	4	7	1	3
6	9	5	8	4	3	1	2	7
4	8	2	1	6	7	5	3	9
7	3	1	9	5	2	8	4	6

6 1. Surprise / 2. Joy
3. Anger / 4. Anxious
5. Fear / 6. Suspicious
7. Satisfied / 8. Annoyed

7 Number 3: 6
Number 7: 7

8 1: c / 2. a / 3. a

9 c

10 Part 1: 8 / Part 2: c

11 a. 8 / b. 16 / c. 18

16th session
Brain Exercises

1 a. 1350 / b. 100/32
c. 144 / d. 34 / e. 3300

2 1.you pays your money and you takes your choice 2.Those who cannot learn from history are doomed to repeat it. / 3.The shoemaker's son always goes barefoot 4.The grass is always greener on the other side of the fence

4 Number of "G/g": 13
Number of "S/s": 46

5

(crossword grid with entries: TAN, ALA, CUBE, FETA, ALEC, PRUNE, INTESTINE, ANTES, LEI, OHENRY, TSP, ETC, DENY, ANGE, MAN, WHIRRS, HIVE, ALSO, PACTS, AKIN, ERR, HUEY, DELTA, GONG, APPS, ALOHAS, RIM, ARAB, ERIC, ROM, RUG, SCRAPE, AMI, TRESS, ANTEDATES, EGRET, SITS, RENT, ESPY, KEY, TDS)

6 18

7 a. 24 / b. 7 / c. Third person

8 a. Simon / b. 23
c. 43

9 a. 2 / b. 5

10 4

Extra Exercises

1 a. 3/1 / b. 5 / c. 57
d. 500 / e. 560 / f. 555

2 a. March comes in like a lion and goes out like a lamb / b. One half of the world does not know how the other half lives c. opportunity never knocks twice at any man's door

3 Part 1: b / Part 2: c
Part 3: a

4

(crossword grid with entries: IRISH, ACT, ATMS, DONEE, LIE, SNAPE, OPERA, SAM, ATLAW, LESOTHO, PELICAN, NEE, ATOM, COP, DRAB, NOBODY, LURK, DRAM, NOSEE, ATON, SINUS, BABA, SEMIS, ADDA, SKIS, PROTON, OSLO, ATT, LOON, TRA, EASTERN, EYELASH, ALARM, SAD, GOTTA, REMAN, EGG, ONEIL, LEES, TOE, NEEPS)

7 a

9

3	×	1	+	5	=	8
×		+		−		
4	×	8	−	3	=	29
−		−		×		
9	×	6	÷	2	=	27
×		×		×		
5	+	3	−	7	=	1
+		÷		−		
4	×	9	÷	6	=	6
=		=		=		
19		1		22		

10 Part 1: b / Part 2: a

12 Part 1: a / Part 2: a
Part 3: c

www.ingramcontent.com/pod-product-compliance
Lightning Source LLC
LaVergne TN
LVHW051515070426
835507LV00023B/3120